Ouija Board

How to Use a Ouija Board

(Fascinating Experiences With the Mysterious Spirit Oracle)

Arthur Jones

Published By **Oliver Leish**

Arthur Jones

All Rights Reserved

Ouija Board: How to Use a Ouija Board (Fascinating Experiences With the Mysterious Spirit Oracle)

ISBN 978-1-77485-566-9

No part of this guidebook shall be reproduced in any form without permission in writing from the publisher except in the case of brief quotations embodied in critical articles or reviews.

Legal & Disclaimer

The information contained in this ebook is not designed to replace or take the place of any form of medicine or professional medical advice. The information in this ebook has been provided for educational & entertainment purposes only.

The information contained in this book has been compiled from sources deemed reliable, and it is accurate to the best of the Author's knowledge; however, the Author cannot guarantee its accuracy and validity and cannot be held liable for any errors or omissions. Changes are periodically made to this book. You must consult your doctor or get professional medical advice before using any of the suggested remedies, techniques, or information in this book.

Upon using the information contained in this book, you agree to hold harmless the Author from and against any damages, costs, and expenses, including any legal fees potentially resulting from the application of any of the information provided by this guide. This disclaimer applies to any damages or injury caused by the use and application, whether directly or indirectly, of any advice or information presented, whether for breach of contract, tort, negligence, personal injury, criminal intent, or under any other cause of action.

You agree to accept all risks of using the information presented inside this book. You need to consult a professional medical practitioner in order to ensure you are both able and healthy enough to participate in this program.

TABLE OF CONTENTS

Introduction 1

Chapter 1: History Of Talking Boards 9

Chapter 2: Game Of Ouija Explained 32

Chapter 3: The Haunting Information Regarding The Ouija Board & Ouija Faq . 41

Chapter 4: Ouija: Not Exactly The Game 59

Chapter 5: Devil Ouija Board Spells That Live Even Despite Attempts To Ward They Off 62

Chapter 6: Jane Roberts, Seth, The Parker Brothers, & Others 67

Chapter 7: Faith Or Religious Doesn't Protect You Against Ouija Board Spirits . 73

Chapter 8: Young People And Their Experiences Using The Ouija Board 76

Chapter 9: The Collection Of Short Ouija Board Horror Stories 86

Chapter 10: Celebrity Ouija Board Account Over The Years 93

Chapter 11: Decoding The Different Possession Accounts And Other Similar Patterns 101

Chapter 12: Ouija And Its Haunting Powers 122

Chapter 13: Skepticism About Talking Boards.. 134

Chapter 14: Famous People Consulting Ouija 157

Chapter 15: What To Do With An Ouija Board 172

Conclusion 182

Introduction

Ouiji (pronounced wee-ji) or Ouija board. Ouiji (pronounced "wee-ji") also known as Ouija board also known as a talking board, or spirit board, is an unfinished flat board decorated with the letters of the alphabet, numbers ranging from 0 to 9 as well as the words yes as well as no, and sometimes even hello. Additionally it also has a variety of other symbols and pictures.

It utilizes a planchette which is a tiny piece of wood heart-shaped. In recent years plastic has been used instead of wood planchettes. The Planchettes slide through each other on an Ouija board to write phrases.

Commercial Introduction

Many people believe that Elijah Bond invented the Ouija Board in 1890, the reality is the Ouija board existed long before 1890. Actually, anyone who tries to claim that the Ouija was invented in 1890 is left with a lot of research to complete. Although the Ouija isn't new, Elijah Bond only introduced it to the market in 1890. It's not surprising to discover that Mr. Bond was a mere businessman.

At the time the board was little more than a game and a game that was mystical in appearance, was entertaining more than any other thing. In the past, Ouija was simply an enjoyable game for the parlor, and was not connected to the supernatural.

There followed World War I and with it came a man who would forever alter the way that people looked at the Ouija as a Spiritualist Pearl Curran, the man who popularized the Ouija board as a divining instrument.

In the 1880s, spiritualists believed that once the loved ones died, the spirit of that person was still able to contact the living. They had a board which was like the modern Ouija board, and claimed that it "made the communication with spirits much faster." What does Christians, Occultists and Scientists have to say about this board in the end? Is it spiritual is it? Let's look:

Christians and Their View in the Ouija Board

Christians around the globe oppose people who use the Ouija board. The battle against the Ouija board is fiercest in the West which is where its usage is at its highest. Christian religious groups have highlighted the board as extremely hazardous and its use could give way to the possession of demons.

Occultists and their opinions about the Ouija Board

The opinion of occultists on this topic is differs. Some believe that it can result in "positive transformation" but other occultists seem to have sided with Christians. They have added a new element to their argument by calling for "inexperienced" players to avoid the board and instead find a different toy for them to play with.

Scientists are Their Say on the Ouija Board

Scientists have adopted their own stance which mainly focuses on criticizing both the occultists and the Christians. Scientists have made it a habit of slamming the beliefs of both sides by describing their beliefs to be "pure false science."

What is the reason we included the three arguments we have throughout this book? It depends on who you are and what your background is you could fall in any of the three groups. Yes, there's an undefined gray zone If you are a member of this group then you're probably doubtful about the Board's "powers" however, you aren't totally sceptical of them.

To help you comprehend the board in greater detail and better, let's dig deep into its past.

The History of Ouija Board

The Ouija board employs the spiritual method of communication called "automatic writing" (there are a few scattered of references to that specific word.) One of the first mentions of the automated writing technique used on the Ouija board dates the origins of this method to Ancient China in the year 1100 AD.

How can we be sure of this? The Chinese are extremely adept in preserving their past (Asians generally excel in that kind of thing, anyway) and the documents from the history from the famed Song Dynasty show this method of writing automatically.

The technique was and isknown as "Fuji." In translation into English, Fuji refers to "planchette writing." The method of writing with planchettes to facilitate communication with spirits was practiced throughout the ages, and though there were changes, as well as the appearance of new ways to communicate via spirits, the original method was able to continue. It was only following the creation by the Qing Dynasty that Fuji use was halted after the dynasty had banned the practice.

There are a lot of Scriptures devoted to this automatic writing technique. One of the authors of these scriptures asserts that similar methods of spiritual writing were commonplace throughout Greece, Rome, Ancient India and Medieval Europe. When you examine this, you realize that the Ouija is a bit of historical background.

Talking Boards and the Ouija Board

The 19th century was when spirituality became popular. Many wanted to be in contact with spirits of their deceased loved loved ones. In addition, they wanted more effective methods of communication with spirits than the ones currently available.

This demand led to the development of "talking boards" which more or less were based on the same idea like the boards of the Song Dynasty. In 1886, four years prior to the time that Elijah Bond introduced the Ouija board to the world as commercial packages The talking boards became so widespread that, at some point, they became frequently featured in news reports. The news report said, "The board has truly revolutionized the world of spirituality." Ohio was especially loved by the Ouija board.

The Game in the Commercial Parlor That became known as the Ouija Board

Before we go to the subject, it is important to understand that even though the first patent filing to create this Ouija board was completed in 1890, the Ouija board, or, at a minimum the concept behind it, is much more dated than that. Patents have a purpose, but are they not? That's why claiming that"the Ouija board was invented in 1890 gives you an answer even though you're not completely correct.

Businessman Elijah Bond had the idea to patent the planchette. Keep this in mind and take it in your heart The planchette was the object of the patent. The board was merely an item that was included with the planchette.

The patent was sold with a wooden board with an alphabet written. The idea, as stated by Elijah Bond, heavily borrowed from talking boards previously used. Patentees were quick to submit the patent application on the Ouija board. On May 28, 1890, the Ouija board was granted patent protection. This is the reason until today, Bond and company get credit for the creation of this Ouija board. The fact that the patent attorney was an Elijah Wood did not hinder Elijah Wood's cause.

Evidently, many were not happy - and continue to be unhappyabout the "reinvention of the past" with regard to how the board's actions were concerned. This may be the reason William Fuld, Elijah Bond's employee, was able to spend a significant portion of his time litigating against several businesses regarding the Ouija board following his takeover from Bond.

Chapter 1: History Of Talking Boards

In the year 1848 something strange occurred in the lodge of Hydesville, New York lodge. The two sisters Kate as well as Margaret Fox discovered the spirit of a deceased vendor, and became instant celebrities and sparked a nationwide fixation that spread throughout all of the United States and Europe. It was the birthplace of cutting-edge Spiritualism.

The whole world was eager to communicate with the deceased. Mystic chapels were popping up everywhere and those who had the unique gift as a "pipeline" towards"the "next direction" were of great interest. These extraordinary individuals, designated "mediums" due to their ability to move around as delegates between spirits and other people, developed various intriguing ways to connect to the soul realm. The table turning (tilting or tipping) was just one of them. The medium and coming to sitters would lay their hands on the table and then hold their hands tightly for intense contact. The table would sway and shift in a thumping motion on the floor to letters from the set of letters. The entire messages of the spirits were written out in this line.

An alternative that was less controversial was a kind of soul writing using an wicker container that was small and an unattached pencil at the other end. The medium had to get in touch with the wicker container and establish contact, and then the soul would take over, creating messages through to the Great Beyond. The pencil wicker vessel advanced into the heart-shaped planchette, an even more elaborate device, with two casters that turn underneath and a pencil on the end, which was used to shape an additional leg. Mystics quickly discovered that, in addition to the ability to compose messages the planchette could function as a pointer, thereby setting an example for discussion sheets to follow. Kate Field composed, "Significant W. Would like to know his wife's name. He I gave me a list of 13 names. After three attempts

Planchette pointed out the one that was right." --Planchette's Diary, 1868. According to some journalists that the person who designed the planchette was an incredibly well-known French medium called M. Planchette. It is not possible since there is no information on this person is available and"planchette" is a French phrase "planchette" refers to English meaning "little boards."

Many of your customers may want to talk with their soul mates, however, they might not be able to use that mediumistic force, which is usually thought of as the first step or the beginning of progress in mediumistic terms through the capacity to give by tipping the table. However it was discovered by my wife the method that can allow individuals to obtain indications that they aren't able to receive tipping at the table and for those who have to tip the table in order to draw attention to the letters whenever the set of letters is called, a method is provided to increase the efficiency of operations. My wife and I, have discovered that we (not independently) could to have sexual relations with soulmates through tipping, found the process extremely monotonous, but when we tried the new approach, our soul child yelled: "Goodness dear daddy and mom, you've made my work so easy in this moment." The procedure is as follows The method is: I've at the table, painted the letters of the alphabet set. Then on this table , we have the pole that is clean, that is adjusted beneath and pointed at both closures. The top side is large enough for fingers to rest and is also hard so that they don't fall off. The table must be extremely smooth. I encourage the operation by placing a cleanser stone that is powdered. On this pole , the fingers of the two individuals that are seated on opposite sides are placed and the bar can be allowed to glide across the letters. This way we have received messages quicker than we did by writing. If you consider this article is useful, readers are invited to read take it. Yours in perpetuity. LK American Spiritualist Magazine, December 18, 1876.

American as well as European toy manufacturers successfully promoted the planchette and made it hugely prominent. Dial plate devices although more complicated were to a large degree ignored. This was due to the fact that they were much easier to manufacture and sell as unusual items. They both had a rearward-facing sitting arrangement in 1886, when news of a rousing new "talking board" sensation swept the magazine kiosks. In the March 28th Sunday edition in The New York Tribune, the report quickly spread throughout the nation. This is a reprint the Tribune article from The Carrier Dove, an Oakland, California publication for Spiritualists, The Carrier Dove:

THE NEW PLANCHETTE.

~~~~~~~

A Mysterious Talking Table and Table.

~~~~~~~

"Planchette is a complete shambles," said a Western man at the Fifth Avenue Hotel, "compared to the latest scheme of obscure communication being tested in Ohio. I have heard of entire communities who are in awe of the "talking board," as they refer to it. I've not heard of the term "talking board" in any way. But I've seen and heard about some of the most fascinating aspects of its operation. Things that appear to transcend human understanding and explanation."

"What does the board look like?" "Give me the pencil and I'll give you. The first requirement is an operating board. It can be rectangular, averaging 18x20 inches. The inscribed text reads: "The 'yes' and the 'no' serve to initiate and conclude the conversation. Good-night and good-evening are reserved for good manners. A small table that is that is three or four inches in height is built using four legs. Anyone can construct the entire device in 15 minutes with two scissors and a marker brush. The board is placed on your lap, and another who is sitting next to you. Each of you holds the table with your thumb and forefinger in each corner to the side. Then you are asked "Are there any messages?' Sooner or later, you realize that another person has been pushing you around. He is convinced that you are making the same move. However, the table is moved to say 'yes' or 'no.' You continue to ask questions and the responses are clearly written through the table's legs sitting over the alphabet one letter after another. Sometimes, the table covers two letters by dragging its feet, then you hold on to it and request for the table to be removed from the incorrect letter. This is accomplished. A few remarkable conversations have repeated until people have become of awe about the subject. I know of a man who's family became so involved by the whole witching doll that he decided to burn it. That same night, he set off leaving town for an business trip. His family members tried to locate the board, but were unable to locate it. They enlisted a helper to create another one. Then , two of the guests sat down and inquired what happened to the table they had previously sat at. The answer was given with a name "Jack burnt it..' There's, of course, plenty of absurd and unrelated answers given, but the employees pay little pay attention to these. If the answers are pertinent, they debate them over with a sense of admiration. A friend of mine informed me that he received an announcement about the title to a property from his deceased brother and that it was of huge significance to him. It's interesting as per those who been working most closely with the mystery, that even though two people are sitting at the table, a third in the same room a far away, could ask questions without saying them out loud and the responses will be revealed to the person sitting behind them. Also, the answers will be given to the queries of one of the people working, whereas the other will receive no responses at all. The planchette is in Youngstown, Canton, Warren, Tiffin, Mansfield, Akron, Elyria, and several other cities in Ohio I have heard there was a fervor regarding the new planchette. Its operation and use have been able to replace cards in the form of. It is attempted to verify claims given about living people and, in some instances, they have been successful so that they leave the inquirers further astonished. "--New York Times.

-- Carrier Dove (Oakland) July, 1886: 171. The image is reprinted in the New York Daily Tribune, March 28th 1886: page 9, column 6. "The New "Planchette.' A Strange Talking Board and Table Over Which Northern Ohio is Agitated."

This was quite remarkable because the "new" communication board seemed simple to construct and needed no understanding or expertise. It was also not planning to accomplish, or at least in the vicinity , the people were instructed to access it. When the marker "moved independently of anyone else" from letters to letters to establish the message, it appeared like a mystical and baffling. Maybe this was a different innovation. However what would you say that it was? At the exact same time one of the nation's most prolific toy makers, W. S. Reed Toy Company located in Leominster Massachusetts, put out an item that resembled that of the "new Planchette." It is unclear if this was an answer to or responsible for the rage, we'll guess. It was dubbed"the "witch board" it was described as that: "Upon the four sides of the board are the words "Yes," "No," "Great by" and "Great day,"" and the letter set is the central point on the table. A miniature table, resting on four legs, is placed on the "witch board" which is where the hands are placed, and then the spirits begin their work. If the answer is "Yes" or "No," the little table will move to the corner that is individual and vice versa. Interchanges are written out on the small table, which rests on the letters that are required to express the message.--Boston Globe, June 5 1886

Reed's brief "witch board" could have been completely missed if not to be a rousing story. Charles S. Dresser, Reed's treasurer sent the president Grover Cleveland one of them as an offering to the couple with the intention that "it could be an administration item." If Dresser could have been playing with the wedding is a matter of speculation. Frances Folsom was 27 years younger than President, and the difference in age between them set the world on the edge. Cleveland replied with a kind smile "I apart from it being an affirmation of my feelings and kinship, and appreciate its resilience but I'm not certain that I'd be able to immediately check its strength to uncover the past and anticipate the future to follow."

While Reed didn't patent a similar item such as the Espirito up to 1891, other investors were on the board trend in just only a few days. The primary patent to "changes," documented on May 28, 1890, and granted the following day, February 10, 1891 runs down Elijah J. Bond as the one who invented the invention and appointed for the patent as Charles W. Kennard and William H. A. Maupin from Baltimore, Maryland. The question of what Bond as well as his Baltimore friends thought of Reed's earlier "witch board" is according to what the board might declare, unclear, however it is clear of their being the first people to develop the board as an unusuality.

Charles Kennard stated that he named the new board Ouija (pronounced we-ja) after a discussion of discussion with Miss Peters, Elijah Bond's sister-in-law "I said that we hadn't yet come up with a name and considering that the board had assisted us in many other ways, we decided to suggest a name. The board spelled out O-U.I.J-A. When I inquired about what the meaning behind the word was, it read 'Good Luck.' Miss Peters then drew on her neck an ornamental chain, which was finished with the locket. On it was the figure of a woman and on top of it the word "Ouija'. Then we inquired if they had considered the word and she told us that she hadn't. Then we adopted the name. The presenters were Mr. Bond as well as his wife, daughter, Miss Peters and myself." Kennard and Bond, doing business under the name Kennard Novelty

Company, wasted nothing advertising in local publications:

"The Ouija"

THE Wonder of the NINETEENTH Century

The most fascinating and intriguing Talking Board has sparked great curiosity everywhere it has been it was shown. It is superior in its results to second sight and mind reading, also known as clairvoyance. It is a small table that is placed on a huge board that contains the alphabet and numbers. When you place your fingers on two people on the table it is moved, and for the best of its ability, it becomes an intelligent living thing, providing precise answers to any question which can be formulated. As amazing as it may sound it is not the case "Ouija" was rigorously test and the above data was were demonstrated in the United States patent office before the patent was approved. It is available for purchase to all first-class Toy Dealers and Stationers. Produced through The Kennard Novelty Company,

220 South Charles street, Baltimore, Md.--
Baltimore Sun, December 6, 1890.

Charles Kennard left the company after 14 months, and founded Northwestern Toy Company in Chicago, Illinois. The ex-financial partners of his, led by the powerful Baltimore Capitalist Washington Bowie, who was also manager, secretary as well as treasurer for Kennard Novelty, continued the business under corporate control. They changing its name for the company as Ouija Novelty Company. The name change didn't affect Kennard who developed his best-known product the Volo board, which was a Ouija replica. Bowie immediately brought suit against the patent for infringement, which led to the demise of the Volo and a somewhat embarrassing apology by Northwestern to the industry. Indefatigable, Charles Kennard continued in real estate and in other business ventures, and also created another talking board called the Igili in 1897.

Perhaps Kennard's sense of privilege stemmed in his role as the creator of the Ouija board. A series of letters sent directed to Baltimore Sun in 1919, insistently addressing the issue. Kennard wrote his own design and been able to (the period of rage over talking boards) constructed rough boards, using cake boards as well as an elongated table and a pointer. He then engraved in pencil the letters number and set. The office that he was in was run by an cabinet maker by the name of E.C. Reiche who, on the request of Kennard, produced several copies from the plank. When asked to create these in large numbers for commercial use, Reiche cannot, whining of a hefty work load. Following a search around Baltimore and not finding any buyers, Kennard met Elijah Bond who made a few modifications such as the semi-round letters in order layout and the extension of felt pads on leg of the pointer, and also was able to license the upgrades. Bond was then joined by Kennard to create Kennard Novelty

Company. Kennard Novelty Company name.

Elijah Bond sided with Kennard however he stated that it was Bond, Bond, who had created the company and held complete control, as he was the largest shareholder. He referred to it as Kennard Novelty in "compliment towards Kennard.. Kennard." Bond added that he'd traveled for a trip to Washington with a woman (Helen Peters) who was who was a "strong medium" and had astonished one of the top officials of the Patent Office. the chief then assured him that his patent was going to be approved. Similar patents from Canada, England, and France were granted. Bond acknowledged Kennard for bringing Ouija to his notice and possessing the zeal and capacity to help make the board an instant success. After a trip to London and failing to utilize the benefits of his English Patent in 1892 Bond found himself forced to sell his shares and surrender his stake in the company.

Washington Bowie questioned Kennard on some numbers. He stated that the inventor of the Ouija wasn't Charles Kennard but rather Mr. E. C. Reiche of Chestertown, Maryland. He added the fact that Kennard Novelty required Reiche in cash to allow "utilizing his work without compensation" and that this occurred not just once, but two times, Reiche being malcontented with the first settlement. E. C. Reiche's son, W. Mack Reiche was a staunch supporter of Washington Bowie and permitted that even though Kennard might have called the Ouija however he never actually invented the device. It was his opinion that Kennard did not even think of a device like this until it was revealed to him in the house of judge Joseph A. Wickes, Kennard's father in law. W. Mack Reiche was not apprehensive to the idea that Ouija "started to operate via the brain and hands of father and son alone."

No matter what the tale, Washington Bowie remained the central figure in his company Ouija Novelty Company settling on the majority of corporate decisions, and also the introduction of his son, Washington Bowie Jr. as the chief for the Chicago production plant. The moment he arrived he took 20-year aged William Fuld under his wing and taught him everything could be taught about business. Fuld was quickly promoted to the post of foreman, and later to become one of the initial shareholders of the company. The year was 1897. Washington Bowie rented the rights to create Ouija boards. Ouija board for William and his brother Isaac. In that one fateful event, William Fuld came to be the person that history will forever remember as the creator of the Ouija board.

William as well as Isaac Fuld left effectively on their new venture and released Ouija sheets in record-breaking number. Then, the business relationship did not last long. Ouija Novelty's deal in The Fulds were for a lengthy period of time. At the close of this time, William shaped his own specific organization and ended the association and Isaac's right to form the Ouija board was also completed. A legal battle ensued following. The sharpness led to a serious family feud that would persist for several various eras. Isaac was a home-based workshop, where he dispensed as well as sold Ouija copied, called Oriole talking sheets, as well as smoking and pool tables. Ouija Novelty earned revenue on its Ouija Name through William Fuld and after that in 1919, the company surrendered its remaining rights. William was the seller of a lot of Ouija sheet, toy as well as other games, and maintained the position of an US traditional examiner. A few years later, the man became one of Baltimore's General Assembly.

For the past 26 decades William Fuld ran the organization through turbulent times and great ones. When he first came across information with regard to the Ouija the man was humorously honest. He was an Presbyterian and didn't believe that it was a method of communication with spirits left behind but at the same time believed of the Ouija was a good adviser for personal and professional life. The explanation he gave was that the Ouija board by an attraction, or a sense of wonder, guided the hands and gave to give the appropriate responses. He shared personal stories to clarify. The board advised Fuld to "plan for massive business" and Fuld did so, constructing another industrial facility to meet the huge demand. When an enormous shipment that was sent for St. Paul, Minnesota went missing, and railroad officials did not find it. Fuld sought for the Ouija board for guidance and it led him to Ohio and right to the point where it was misled. "The Ouija board was announcing itself." He added. "We were unsure of how to call it, so put the question on the board, and it spells out O-U-IJ-A. We had no idea of what it meant, so we scratched for quite some time before we found any clue. Finally, we discovered it was a rough speculation that came from an Egyptian word that signified luck." Even though "innovator" was printed across the bottom of every boards, William Fuld didn't claim to be the inventor. He acknowledged E. C.

Reiche but claimed that he had taken a shot at a comparable board, and was knocked down by Patent Office.

On February 19, 1927 William Fuld moved to the highest point in his Harford Street plant in Baltimore to supervise the replacement of the flagpole. A bolster pole was his holding broke and he fell backwards until his death. Following his death William's children took over and promoted a myriad of fascinating Ouija versions that they could make their own, such as the rare and exquisite Art Deco Electronic Mystifying Oracle. In the year 1966, they resigned and transferred the business in the hands of Parker Brothers. Parker Brothers created a precise generation and swiftly created an exquisite Maple Deluxe Wooden Edition Ouija.

From the very beginning point William Fuld's Ouija board was a target of fierce competition with other creators of toys. Everyone wanted to create several variations from variations of Wonderful

Talking Board. Ouija imitations with names like "The Wireless Messenger" and I Do Psycho Ideograph, have flooded the market. Certain organizations, like J.M. Simmons or Morton E. Chat & Son even used the Ouija name and indistinguishable board's design. Fuld was able to respond with lawful threats and also promoted a second smaller, more modest talking board called the Mystifying Oracle.

The 1940s were a collection of imaginative and vibrant talking sheets. Perhaps the most enjoyable were the Haskelite's Egyptian theme Mystic Boards and Mystic Trays. The other real players were two Chicago oddity organizations: Gift Craft, and Lee Industries. With all kinds of wizards and wild animals, these talk sheets were a great reinterpretation of Fuld's number sheets that were the basis of his. Blessing Craft's famed Swami featured flying carpets and a genii advising the gem ball. Lee's Magic Marvel, done in beautiful yellow and red included four diviners in turbans as well as the zodiac and some mysterious evil spirits that were tossed in for good luck. You can either love them or not they aren't exhausting.

In the middle of 1999, Parker Brothers quit fabricating the superb Fuld Ouija board and then changed to a lessand gritty, shiny, oblivious design. The false elevated maple lithograph, and gone was that name: William Fuld. Although a few might mourn its loss but we should remember it's Parker Brothers motto: "It's an excuse to say?"

Chapter 2: Game Of Ouija Explained

Does this book suggest the use of a board? It definitely does not. However, if going to be reading the horror stories and tales that be included in the next chapters it is important to know the basics of how you can play the Ouija.

It's a link to many other things that we'll discuss later. Furthermore is that you won't be reading up on terrifying accounts and shaking, while you have only a hazy notion of what the game is. You will be able to be able to comprehend the Ouija.

In the end, deciding whether or not play the Ouija is up to you. However, from the stories you'll learn in the book you will be able to discern what the author's beliefs are on whether or not you should not participate in the Ouija.

Let's start with the beginning:

A Ouija Board is an elongated, smooth surface made from wood and has the letters A-Z, the numbers between 0-9 and the moon and sun symbol printed on. It also has a moveable indicator, called the planchette, that is which is used to answer any questions asked by the person using the.

Ouija board Ouija board was extremely popular during the 1920s as well as in it's World War I period. It's not difficult to understand why people lost a lot of their loved ones during the war, and clearly enjoyed talking to them.

It was the perfect soil that was perfect for the Ouija board, and in a flash, people were able to communicate to their spirit. The Ouija board's marketing was smart in its own right with such abstract terms such as "the most effective method to communicate with your deceased loved one" wouldn't have had any appeal.

However, advertising it as an "spiritual connection; a method to connect with the dead" was a hit and attracted a large number of people. This was a board that talked that was not overhyped, yet, the rumours about the board proclaimed its efficacy. People were buying Ouija boards the moment they were on the shelves of stores.

Learn how to utilize the board:

Utilizing the Board

Utilizing the Ouija board, there are three components to it:

The First Part: Creating Ambience

Here's how you can establish the mood:

Find a partner Technically, you can play the Ouija by yourself. However, it's more enjoyable when playing with a partner because of two reasons. The one is the fear factor, and the second reason, that is more logical being that a seasoned hand will assist you in getting the essence of Ouija quicker.

Two people is the ideal numbers or players. If there are too many people, the situation will appear to be all over the place. Mediums often disapprove of from having too many individuals saying that it could "confuse spirits" which could be true.

Make sure you are in a good mood: You'll perform this in the traditional way (which is actually the only method). Burn incense should you have it. But, you don't require burning incense when playing Ouija because dimming the light and lighting a few candles can usually establish the mood.

It is believed that playing the Ouija could be about timing. Sometimes the Ouija will lie in bed, "asleep." Other times, it's extremely responsive. Mediums suggest that you use the Ouija in the evening, or even in the early hours of the day.

In order to set the mood, you must eliminate any distracting factors. If you prefer to play your hi-fi system for 24 hours per day it is best to unplug it to enjoy the music. Mobile phones can also disrupt the connection between spirits. It is best to keep them in the other room.

Sit down: The original instructions require that the board be placed on participant's knees. It also requires the presence of a "lady and gentleman." So, consider these guidelines for what they are. But, it won't hinder the process if you put the board on a table or a floor that is clean.

2. Part 2: Proper Mindset in Ouija

It is important to understand that playing the Ouija is a game that has a mental component to it. To participate in the game it is necessary to have the right mental state. Here's how you can cultivate the right mindset

The patience: Members of the board say that at times it is necessary to keep the spirit warming up. Don't ask how. it's just a matter of. You can ask questions to the spirit may not be in a flash.

However, this book should help you understand In the book, you will find that suggestions such as, "Move the planchette a little" in order to get it warm are complete nonsense. This myth has no meaning. The spirit is the one who can provide the answers and instead of the planchette.

Politeness: The idea here is that if dealing with a character that is extremely communicative, you should talk to it the same way as you would to a friend you've known for a long time. If you're keen on formalities and pleasantries take advantage of it. It helps the soul to be more open. Similar to this when the spirit is making incredibly long stops between answers, remain respectful and avoid using expletives and the use of profanity.

The first step is that you shouldn't bombard your audience with at the same time. Think of it as an ordinary conversation, which means beginning slow and moving from there.

Be cautious about what you want to happen The most damaging ways to live is to spend a long time in a row while contemplating your imminent death. It's sure to bring trouble when you contemplate what you might do.

Is that motor vehicle speeding on the highway be able to kill you quickly or get you to your ER first? Do the gangly knife-wielding youngster and blind alley be able to make it fast or will he struggle in his task? If you're not sure about the right answer for a query, you should stay far from asking the question. In addition, why would you ask spirit questions , such as "Does Moses' little sibling have a similarity to me?"

The Third Part is playing the Game

To take part in the game:

Choose a medium. This is simply to choose a person to be the one to ask questions. This makes things easier.

Fingers on the planchette For the first time the planchette should be placed in the "G place on the piece of paper. Everyone should gently put their index and middle fingers onto the planchette. Next, focus on what you would like to inquire about. Your fingers should be placed with a firm grip, but not to the point that you force that your fingers are hurting.

Create your own opening ritual This could be something you choose. You could chant a lengthy mantra to establish the tone, or throw trinkets on the floor. Whatever is appealing to you Do it.

Let your medium welcome the spirits and declare that the only type of energy you will receive on this morning is positivity. If you're keen on speaking to a deceased relative Have the deceased relatives be in close proximity.

Ask: Start with a set of easy questions. Then, you move forward until you feel comfortable with the flow of the discussion. If the spirit suggests that the person is dark then the best option is to put the board down and then return afterward. If you get vulgar responses, do not dish it right back.

Concentrate: To receive optimal results from the mind everyone will have to be focused on the training sessions and unwind their minds.

Watch it move. By watching it move, we're being able to watch the planchette change. Sometimes, it will move at a rapid pace, and at other times, it'll move slow. There will be instances where it sits still.

Shut the board down If the planchette begins playing ladders and snakes across the table, the countdown goes from 9 to zero before washing it off and repeating it, it's time to stop your séance by shifting the planchette away.

If you experience this, it typically signifies that the spirit of your loved ones is trying to get away from from the board. Mediums also emphasize that you tell your spirit farewell. When asked about this they usually reply by saying "well you'd hate it if someone with whom who you were speaking to abruptly quit, wouldn't you?"

We now have a better understanding of the Ouija board. are now ready to move on to the spooky section that is that Ouija board. The first step is to understand some scary facts about the board prior to proceeding to the spooky stories.

Chapter 3: The Haunting Information Regarding The Ouija Board & Ouija Faq

Your fascination with the Ouija board probably stems from the numerous haunting stories of people who play the game. Let's take a look at some interesting facts about Ouija board:

Unsettling Information concerning the Ouija Board

The details are here to give you greater insight into the boards. In a few instances you'll get information that will aid you in understanding the accounts of horror that are included in the book.

1. Jury Uses the Ouija Board To Find a defendant guilty

It was 1994, and the event was a sentencing. Four jurors were present and sitting on their knees was an Ouija board. One juror requested the Ouija board to answer "Who did this?" The board and the jurors in turn, determine the defendant, Mr. Andrew Young, the 35-year-old defendant, guilty of murdering two newlyweds. The verdict seemed unshakeable until the details about the Ouija session became public. The court gave the accused Mr. Young a retrial, but it was not of any assistance to him as, yet again the jury found the defendant guilty.

2. Is the Ouija Board An Accomplice To Multiple Murders?

It is commonplace to hear murderers share their version of events and then say something like "the board told me to commit the crime." The frequency of this is truly alarming. Consider this particular case as an example.

In 2001, the former Minco, Oklahoma, Mayor and Mayor. Brian's wife killed the man in his sleep. She used an kitchen knife and fatally cut the victim. If asked the reason for her actions she replied that the Ouija board said she was required to commit the crime and that Roach was a villain that needed to be killed.

In 2014, a man named Mr. Paul Carroll killed the family dog. He was convinced that during a séance with the Ouija Board, a devil spirit was possessed by his dog. After he had pleaded guilty to a cruelty to animals charge his daughter and wife were convinced that using similar Ouija board was a good idea.

The board members claim that they told them that they would all end up dying. They were compelled to act immediately , and they did. They tore down their house down to the earth. It's unclear whether they burnt the board together with the house.

3 Ouija Board Spells 12 Steps to Recovery

Perhaps you've been familiar with Bill Wilson, the founder of Alcoholics Anonymous. What you might not be aware of is that he used to be a huge lover of the Ouija board. He even had his own area for seances that was spook-filled.

Bill said he utilized the board to connect with a dead 15th century monk called Boniface. His frequent banter with

Boniface is believed to have spawned the well-known 12-step system taught by Alcoholics Anonymous.

4. A Creative Process Gets Spooky

The rock group Mars Volta credits their communication via spirits through an Ouija board to their fourth studio album. The band claims that when they first started using Ouija boards, they discovered poems on it. They were intrigued, and asked for an interpreter, as the poem was written composed in Hebrew in Hebrew and Latin. They even go as to claim that some lines were written in Aramaic.

They claim that the translator they planned to employ refunded their money and clarified that he was not going to meet with the band members or work with them in the future. They sought out an experienced translator to complete the task.

Bixler-Zavala wrote down every word the board said because he thought it was more original than anything ever before. He estimates that it was 10 times more imaginative than any idea they could thought of independently.

However, after a while they realized that the person they were communicating with had caused a tiff in the conversation. One reason was that the studio they were working in was filled with. They were then confronted with a number of terrible equipment problems and the tracks they completed disappeared from their computers "right in front of they could even see."

In addition the drummer left and Bixler-Zavala sprained his foot. The foot injury was serious enough that it required surgery. Rodriguez-Lopez was a band member and decided they had to take care of the board. He destroyed the board and then set about burying the remains in a hidden location. The band members claim that the spirit was still alive. The Digital Version of "The bedlam of Goliath" was released via a flash drive with a unique design of the Ouija planchette.

5. Seances in the White House

Abraham Lincoln and his wife Mary Todd Lincoln lost their son when he was only a few years old. Mary Todd Lincoln got into the habit of having séances in the White House so she could keep in touch with him and connect to his soul.

6. Several Loopholes in the Religious System perpetuate the use for the Ouija Board

You'd think Christians from the past would have gotten on the spirit boards with some energy. This is because, in past times the church was a major factor in the society.

But, did you know that spirits boards and fortunetellers were given minimal interest by the Church? Fortunetellers and spirit boards were given an unrestricted pass, and strict church members would use the boards to connect with ghosts. However, if they didn't perform the task they would search for a medium of the spirit world that would handle the business for them. It is no wonder that spiritual boards endured the religious atmosphere through the centuries.

7. Ghosts and Ouija Boards and Money Streams

In the 1920s the ghost niche became quite popular to the degree that the spiritualist niche was an enticing money-making opportunity. Of course there was more than an equal amount of scammers and smart business people working to make money to the fullest extent they could.

Have a look at Charles Kennard of Baltimore. This was a man who really made hay when sun was shining and rising. He. Kennard pushed a version of the mass-produced spirit boards that became so popular the fledgling firm was able to drop it's "fledgling" classification.

8. The Board Which Patented Itself

According to rumours, when the Ouija board's patenting, many things weren't clear in the Patent Office. The patent office was unable to discern the head and head of "a plaything that could speak on its own."

In the past patents were an important thing. To get a patent you needed to prove a variety of facts regarding your idea. The case of the Ouija board case, the patent office did not seem impressed or convinced. According to rumours, at some moment, Elijah Bond and his group made an arrangement to the patent official. If the board could identify it upon request the patent officer, he would give the patent rights to the name. The officer was willing to grant it.

They requested that the Ouija board name itself after the process of placing the fingertips and mood setting. Lo and behold! The Ouija board pronounced itself by spelling the word "I! Its patent agent was terrified that he rushed ahead and accepted it without the required paperwork for such things.

9: More information on what is the Origin of the Board

Names like "Ouija" has been a major factor for making this board accessible. In addition to the uniqueness in the title, it's very easy to use. When it is mentioned "Ouija," your mind immediately goes to spirit boards.

There is a legend that says the name Ouija is a combination with"oui" from the French "oui" as well as"ja," the German"ja" word "ja," both of which are a synonym for yes. A different legend circulates in the Ouija Chat rooms.

Mystic sister-in-law from one of board members at the business which manufactured Ouija boards, asked to the board, asking the board to choose a name that it liked. The board responded that it believed "Ouija" was an appropriate name. She then asked what the name could mean after which the board responded, "good luck." This is a more interesting story that makes you wonder why everyone is ranting about the French-German name, you ask?

10. The "Ouija Each Home" Policy

You may have heard of you've heard of the Ouija board is a type of board with some gruesome stories about it. It is likely that you'll find a number of accounts in this book. However, throughout it's 100 year (commercial) period the general public saw it in a very different way.

There was a time that Ouija was a popular product. Ouija was a standard product, a cool toy that every family would want to have purchased at some moment. The Ouija was similar to what Newgate Calendar was. Newgate Calendar was in 19th century Britain however that the Ouija board was more calming to gaze at. The more sombre inferences surrounding the Ouija board came later.

Yes, Ouija is a game that Ouija has always been a bit spooky. But, back in the day the perception was of being a "thrillingly scary" game that was it was a source of "comforting entertainment for the citizens." The classic artist Norman Rockwell thought it to be a very noble activity. He described it as the "traditional game that the nation was well-adjusted to accept." In reality the only people who were snoozing on it Ouija game were religious mediums they threw out of their job.

11: Ouija Controversies

When you read this book, you'll discover a number of controversy-filled Ouija accounts. In the meantime Here are some examples:

A factory owner took his own life by jumping off of a structure that he constructed. It was claimed by the owner that the Board given him the instructions to construct the structure. In 1930 in upstate New York, two women murdered their friend following an Ouija board advised them not to kill each other.

There was also the rich woman from Connecticut who, when she died she left her wealth to a ghost who she made a connection with on an Ouija board. The Connecticut court was however refusing to accept that and declared that ghosts was not able to claim any rights for the inheritance.

At the time, Ouija boards were at the very least, rare. They were able to create a board that was "thrillingly creepy." In other words throughout in the 20th and 19th century it was a common sight to watch American families on Saturday evenings huddled around the Ouija board.

12 of Pulitzer Prizes and Ouija Boards

Ouija board Ouija board is believed to be responsible for numerous novels written by writers who claim to have received advice on writing from Ouija board. Ouija board. Consider the case of Pulitzer award-winning poetry writer James Merrill. He attributes his prize-winning poem "Changing light at Sandover" to the sessions which he played using Ouija boards. Ouija board.

13 13. The Ouija Board and "The Exorcist"

Many things have been recognized as the reasons for why the perception of society of the board has changed in this way.

There is nothing that is more worthy of that recognition than the film "The The Exorcist."

The moment the film premiered it was mind-numbing. The acting was phenomenal and the dialogue and acting took us to places that people would rather not go. The show also put the Ouija board in the middle of the proceedings.

In the film the film, a girl plays an Ouija board to communicate with an evil spirit. The spirit takes over her, to the pain of her mother. A priest is a victim of the same and so are the muscles in her neck. The way in which the film presented the board as a way for spirits to connect with the living changed the Ouija board's view forever.

Consolidation of the Bad Rep

The Exorcist got the ball in motion. Over the course of a night, what was an enjoyable cool toy turned into a headline news and the church began strongly disapproving of the company. Few things can advance an idea more than the church and religious organizations and their factions. People began to come out of the woodwork and tell their own personal stories. Some were real and others like you'd imagine, were fiction.

Consistency

The man who said "No publicity is not good publicity" probably at the very least had an eye at Ouija board. Ouija board. It is expected that the negative feedback that the Ouija board was getting to slash sales. If you believe Ouija board sales suffered a decline but you're wrong. This is the proof to prove it: over 120 years of usage, Ouija board sales have been consistent regardless of who bought an ownership right to this board.

What are these figures revealing? First of all you'll now know what the reason why an Ouija board is so widely utilized: at some point in American history the Ouija board was the most common item in every house. It also provides a glimpse instances of "good" things that were derived from spirits that were summoned through using the Ouija board (such as poetry that won awards) and some grisly ones, like the deaths of.

In the stories contained in this book, you'll find similar patterns and the basic Ouija knowledge you've acquired up to now will assist you to process the information. Before we go on we'll first look at some of the answers to commonly asked questions regarding how to use the Ouija board.

Ouija Board Frequently Asked Questions

Like all instruments that need an operating procedure and function, the Ouija board has plenty of frequently-asked questions. But, among these questions, some are frequently repeated. Before we get into the stories, you must have knowledge of these questions since they can aid you in affixing the tales you'll be reading within this collection. They'll add to any way towards your comprehension of Ouija.

In itself an enjoyable story is a good thing however, when you've got information that helps you comprehend it better and to gain more knowledge learning is the main goal of this book.

1. What if the Ouija's Planchette Doesn't Move to Goodbye?

If it doesn't move, the players will need to move it to the new location. Remaining as is cannot be a viable option because it could "leave an open portal." Media insist, is extremely risky.

2. Are Dogs allowed in the Seance?

It's true, this question is often asked and you might wish to know the answer regardless of the motive than to satisfy your curiosity. It is a fact that dogs are a part of séances. But, if the myths of seance are any indication the dogs are highly sensitive to information from the spiritual realm and could have a vision of a spiritual being that could cause an array of barks. This could cause a disturbance to the spirit and end the ritual.

3. If I'm Using my Ouija Board, Will I actually be able to communicate with Ghosts?

The answer is yes enough. You'll be able to be able to communicate with the ghost. It is important to note that the spirit, or ghost should you choose to call it that be able to call it that, will only talk to you via the board. It is at first. However, you should be cautious when use the board-like others you might have encountered in your daily life, ghosts are fraudulent.

4. What Happens Do You Do If The Spirit Refuse to leave?

In light of the fact that this book contains various horror stories You might be interested in knowing what the solution to that question. The solution is to ask the intention to depart in a calm manner. There is also the option to change the planchette so that it says say goodbye. The process, according to the mediums, will end the spiritual connection. You may also perform a spiritual cleansing of the board to cleanse it of any negative energy.

5: What Happens If 21 or any other number Recurres?

It could be a signification of coming to the age of. Perhaps you're trying to communicate something that is related to an upcoming birthday or something that occurred when you were coming to old age. This could be an ominous message aimed to someone who is this particular age.

6: How Do I Stop Getting In Touch With A Bad Spirit?

The legend is that you put one of the silver coins upon the Ouija board. It is believed to help dispel negative spirits. But, it is important to realize that this isn't 100% reliable. Even with a coin of silver put on your body, evil spirits can be able to get through.

Chapter 4: Ouija: Not Exactly The Game

This is the story of a spirit dubbed Angry who became angry and took action to deal with it:

1: David Is Furious

He. Ralph Gold tells a story about how he used the board to convince his friend who was skeptical of the efficacy of the board. It didn't help that there was alcohol in the room, or that the friend was a naive person who spoke in a snarky manner most of the time.

While their hands were on the board and they sat on the board. Ralph Gold knew he was summoning a spirit when the board continued to vibrate. All he had to determine was whether that spirit David is that of a boy who died.

"Are You David?"

It was a yes. Ralph Gold was all too aware of how the board was able to take things in stride and move forward. Gold opened with a new question, but this one was more personal than the previous one.

"At what age did you die when you passed away?"

The spirit indicated "12" as the number. Then, Ralph wrenched his hands off the board and instructed his companion to follow suit. David was, he told his friend who was skeptical was dead at the age of 8, not 12. It was clearly a ghost disguised as David.

Ralph and his companion, who was now throwing a constant stream of insults towards this board. They waited 10 minutes more before taking the board. He was able to get in touch with "David."

David who was playing the board, was able to answer six questions. Ralph requested a seventh, however, before David could respond his question, his friend reacted with a slur that was aimed toward David along with the table. In a flash, the lights inside the room dimmed, and the board slid out of their hands before falling onto the floor.

"You created David mad!" Said Ralph Gold who was furious; his pal laughed at him and suggested they do something else that seemed more sensible, such as to watch TV.

A few hours later, when they headed towards Ralph's vehicle they saw that someone had cut the tires of the car.

"See," said Ralph, "You made David angry and he attacked my tire."

Ralph's friend inquired "If this is the case Why wouldn't David take aim at something I've done because that I'm the person to make him mad?"

"He was chasing me due to the fact that I was the one responsible for summoning him. Even though it was you that angered him but it was me who was responsible for bringing him out in the first place," quipped Ralph.

Chapter 5: Devil Ouija Board Spells That Live Even Despite Attempts To Ward They Off

It's the Ouija board tale of Robert Stamper.

2. Robert Stamper, National Examiner 31787

Robert Stamper tells of how when he was just a few years old he summoned a "foul terror" in his house.

At first, Robert says he and his brother had no luck when they first began making use of this Ouija board. There was then activity. The message indicator began move. Robert explained the movement as "mysterious." First thing that the board informed its users know was "Seth" was relaying information to the board through the board.

Robert along with his son like everyone else and expected, were amazed. And then, Robert, in his own words "made the fatal mistake to tell the panel that he would demonstrate that the event was real , by performing a supernatural feat."

The result, says Robert the author, was "startling and frightening."

The board informed Robert along with his brothers that their grandfather, who was one of closest friends would pass away in about a week. The lighting in the space started shaking violently , and the chimes began to ring in the manner of "pieces of metal being smashed into each other repeatedly."

The room then turned extremely cold, as cold as the ice. Robert along with his son were both shaking from the frigid cold. Another amazing thing, in addition to the incredible severity of the cold was the fact that the thermometer read 70 degrees. A terrible stench of rottenness and death that filled the entire room. It was so strong it was so overwhelming that both boys couldn't stop coughing and gagging.

When began the noises and other disturbances were stopped. The room remained as quiet as a graveyard in the dark of night. The only thing the boys could do was stare at one another, fear in their eyes.

Robert as well as his younger brother leapt into the air and opened their windows in order to ventilate the room and get rid of the foul stench of death. They told each other that it was best to let the entire incident go.

One week later, exactly like it was predicted by the panel that they learned that the father of one of their closest friends passed away. The brothers stared at one another and didn't need to say one word. They were able to recall what the spirit had said. From that point on that chandelier could from time time scream with random rumbling. The smell of decay could be heard throughout the space and temperatures would plummet.

Then, Robert could not take it any more. The board was thrown away and contacted his mom about it all. Robert's mother went straight to the truth. She told her that once you played using an Ouija board, you would be under the negative spell was ad infinitum. Robert ends by writing that, to this day the tremors that shake the house are terrifying. house , and the awful smell of death fills the air.

3. Confessions of Richard"a Spiritual Experimenter'

Richard loved to play with spiritual things. His rule was that the darker, the more mystical. One day when he was at home, he removed the blinds and lit some candles in black before grabbing an Ouija board that he'd amassed. What happened next was quite shocking.

Once he had invoked his spirit, candles went out. In the dim lighting, Richard could see a silhouetted figure cloaked in a cross-legged position to his right. The figure was not visible to the face since the lighting was extremely dim, and the person was wearing an obscured dark cloak that blocked it .

That's how they sat for few minutes: a flesh and blood human being scared to make a move , and an unreal figure who simply stood there. This was when Richard played with the board, or even attempted to test his skills in spiritism. Richard says that the reason he stopped due to "it was pure spooky how the figure with a hood stood there before me, completely motionless and all."

Chapter 6: Jane Roberts, Seth, The Parker Brothers, & Others

This chapter is an assortment of Ouija board game accounts from various players:

4. Jane Roberts & Seth

The second reference Seth receives in the book. Jane Roberts' writings of the 60s and 70s an era when the Ouija board's popularity grew again, are the source of making Seth in the role of an Ouija board-related entity.

Jane Roberts writes that Seth began contact with her through the Ouija board. According to Jane's account the conversation quickly progressed through the various stages. It reached an extent where Seth used pen to talk to Jane before moving further into communication by placing Jane in an euphoria. In this trance Jane states that Seth made use of her vocal cords to communicate.

5. The Ouija Board Usually Summons 'Demons'

In this version, the Sun tells the story:

John Ravens, the head of the family that was afflicted, said, "I believed it may be God himself. The moment the horror was over the blood was literally everywhere, and we all were covered in burn marks that were quite severe. The worst part was that the living room was in chaos."

"It was designed to be a prank," Gloria the wife said. "We were going to with the idea that we were talking to Spirit World."

The two kids and their parents gathered around the Ouija board for a full-on evening of fun. It looked like an evening filled with fun and games. John states that after a bit of period of "playing with it" it was discovered that the "planchette," which lays out what the answer is on the paper began to be able to move itself.

John states that they were all afraid (of obviously they were) However, John was convinced that one of the children was playing with tricks. The kids began asking questions, and the spirit responded with responses. According to John spirits "spoke at us."

"Then," John says, "It asked if it could come to us. At that point I was convinced that somebody was making fun of me, so I said 'yes'"

"The Demon," John narrates, "appeared in just a few minutes. It was a whirlwind of energy and screamed loudly at us and cursing at us. It was clad in a ring of flames and the room became to the point that it became hell. The monster was black and red with bat-like wings, as well as the skin was scaly. It suddenly swooped in and attacked us."

John recalls the demon began with its fangs, pinning them to their faces and arms, and the demon was moving so fast they couldn't get out of the door. The demon kept picking his children and threw the children across the room.

Gloria claims, "It had hooves that got into the faces of my children leaving marks that were very bad."

It wasn't until another hour that affront was over and the spirit dispersed in the same way it had been seen.

6: The Ghost Who simply refuses to leave

Martin an 18-year-old who's gained admiration for Bible and Christianity is a victim of an unrelenting spirit that has afflicted for quite a while. The trouble began when he and his friend played with the Ouija board in the beginning.

Martin claims, "When I used the Ouija board for the first time in my life, a ghost spoke to my girlfriend and me. We were able to talk to the ghost for approximately 7 hours."

"Eventually my girlfriend was asleep. I was trying to remain still around my girlfriend, and so started asking ghost questions in my mind. I just made up the questions, but did not ask them out loud. I was surprised when it had all the answers and that was with out my friend's hand being in the planchette. It was time for me to head to home. I told the spirit that it was not allowed to stay behind me to get back home. But the spirit disobeyed me and continued to follow me."

"That the night that I was there," Martin says, "I was having the worst sleep I've ever had. I was awestruck by this whole experience but. It's the same way that people constantly claim that ghosts and spirits don't exist? They aren't! The ghosts and the spirits exist real as they are! I knew the whole thing out!"

"The issue was that the ghost refused to let me go. It kept me on my toes to no end and demanded that I throw further questions at it. The other thing I noticed was that the lights would flicker around me. I could see glowing colored balls and hear loud sounds that nobody was aware of. It was a bit disturbing at best. Ghosts would also move my body without my having to give it permission and it was not something I would be able to give it consent anyway."

"The ghost was a constant source of chatter. It demanded to continue asking me questions. After a few minutes I had had enough of it. I decided sufficient was enough. This isn't good. I was sure that no GOOD SPIRIT could ever do anything similar to that."

"I called an acquaintance. My friend called me and requested that the spirit be led to the shining light that is Jesus Christ. The ghost listened. The lights stopped blinking around me. But, there was movement in my body. It was only later that I realized that the ghost I saw was merely a mistress for a larger spirit."

(This book will go into detail about the spirits that you summon being extremely stubborn about leaving, as it is usually the case).

Chapter 7: Faith Or Religious Doesn't Protect You Against Ouija Board Spirits

The argument of this section is irrespective of what religion you believe in this chapter does not prove your deity against the supernatural possessions attained through using the Ouija board.

This chapter continues the story of the preceding chapter. It is evident that in this story there is a religious belief that is of a certain kind. But, it doesn't hinder the spirits from causing trouble to the people.

The Ghost Who Refuses To Go (Continued)

"The evil spirit,"" Martin says, "tried to make me worship Satan. Truthfully Prior to this, I didn't consider myself to be a believer in Jesus as well as Satan. I considered them to be myths that have long outlived their place on Earth. The spirit was clear that I could enjoy as much as I desired. The only thing I had to declare was that I was a part of the Satan. This was all I needed to declare. I started begging for Jesus to help me and within me I could feel my spirit start to rage."

"I tried to get rid of this particular spirit," Martin continues, "but this was often a challenge for me. It was so draining that I was prone to slow down at the halfway point. It was the most exhausting thing I've ever been a involved in. My arms would move in a way that was uncontrolled, the back of my neck would get stiffer then the pain grow unbearable. I was unable to endure it."

"At some point I asked the spirit questions, in an effort to determine how I could eliminate it. It was similar to the way investigators question suspects in order to figure out what they're hiding. All for nothing however. In retrospect it was a complete blunder of me to think that I could get a spirit to explaining to me how to eliminate it."

"The spirit was always reminding me of the need the right to murder someone who I love. The last time it informed me this I told it in a direct manner that it would never communicate with me. The only exception occurred in an exorcism."

"Now that I'm conscious that this being that is attached with me has no moral value, I'm looking to have rid of it. I utterly oppose Satan and I totally reject Satan's evil spirit and accept Jesus Christ."

"Deep down I've always believed that I must be snuffed out to be freed from the spirit since I know the spirit that is too for me to get it on my own. Spirit has made it very clear in my mind that it will never quit me. If it refuses to leave, it is to be removed by force."

Chapter 8: Young People And Their Experiences Using The Ouija Board

The Ouija board stories in this chapter were a part of the 1980s and 90s in a mountainous, small town bordered Northern Maine County. The stories vary in severity, but it is evident that there was a price to endure, as evident from the way the victims described the situation.

7: It's Just an Hobby

Cindy was 13 years old, and was the middle child in an enormous, fervent Christian family. She was the oldest of three siblings and two younger ones. One Friday , while she was in the eighth grade, she was able to persuade her friend to loan the girl an Ouija board to use during the weekend.

Over the course of this weekend Cindy as well as her other three siblings enjoyed playing in the Ouija. Since their parents were religious Christians The sisters were extremely cautious and only played with the Ouija board at times which had the lowest risk of being found. This meant they needed to wait until the at odd hours of the night to gather on the table and ask questions.

This week, Cindy was mesmerized to the point of exhaustion. Cindy's fascination with the Ouija was a roaring success (in another chapter, the book will explain the reason of the fascination). Cindy was unable to think of anything that was not connected with the Ouija. She was busy making an agenda of questions she could be asking the board once she was done with the class.

Every day at school, Cindy had an hour in which she was alone at home until her sisters returned to high school. The Monday after her return she went into her room, pulled her Ouija board, set them on their knees and then placed her fingers upon the planschette.

After a period of 10 minutes in this posture, hands placed onto the pointer. The planchette started moving in a jerky manner. It began to spell the word "hi." Cindy gasped. "Hi also," she said, "And who are you?"

"Jake," the Ouija board said. A chill ran through Cindy's body. Jake was her best friend as her grades were lower. Unfortunately, he died in a car crash while the fourth grade was his age.

Cindy stood up. "Jake Is this you?"

At this moment she was shaking with excitement.

The pointer shifted toward "yes" across the table.

Cindy was able to spend the rest of the time with Jake's spirit. Each day after her school she'd hurl into her room and speak to Jake. The conversation would be about everything: from her private life to her plans for the future. However, she noticed that after a few days, conversations got more tense and darker.

In week two, Cindy was convinced that she was talking to Jake's spirit. The same week the spirit would admit to be not Jake however, but it was a demon. It didn't leave the matter there, either. It warned Cindy that she'd die when she shared the conversations they were engaging in. On Friday, after her sisters returned to school, they saw Cindy sitting on the floor crying.

It took her a full one week at a mental facility before Cindy was able to recover from the emotional scars she sustained.

8: You can't keep secrets from Ouija

A hot, summer morning, three young boys stumbled across an Ouija board inside the trash bin of an apartment block. The friendship between these three kids was a complicated one in its own way. Although they were all in love with each other The oldest boy, Tom was known to punch Josh who was the smallest of the three, in the arm.

While he was just engaging into a bit of horseplay, most times however, the punches were powerful enough to cause bruises. He also frequently used his words "retard" as well as "stupid" to cause a rift and hurt Josh.

Chris who was the other child was the other kid who kept his mouth closed. He was not happy with Tom's conduct however, he did not want to create any problems for himself. Therefore, Chris and Josh held some disdain for Tom but loved Tom however, because he spent some time.

In the summer of that year the three boys carried their Ouija game to Tom's home (his parents' house) due to the fact that Tom was always alone for the majority times. His father was at work for a long time while his mother long passed to death. Three boys sat around with the Ouija board, their hands resting in the planchette.

After 20 minutes with nothing happening, they started to feel bored. When they were ready to shift their focus on something else they witnessed something that shocked them all.

A planchette moved. It wrote "Get off" on the ground.

Tom was speaking up. "Get away? What can I do to get away? I'm this place in Christ's name!"

The planchette started moving at velocity, making an 8-figure pattern in the planchette.

It's spelled "Now."

Chris came out, saying, "This is very weird. I'm curious about what all this is about. Where are we going for a change?"

The board wrote "It does hurt."

Chris seemed skeptical. He called the whole process absurd, and instructed Josh to release his grip, believing that he was actually the one who was moving the planchette throughout. Josh put his hands away from the board.

"Ask an inquiry that only you already know about," Tom ordered Josh.

Josh was thinking for a long time before asking "Who is it that tends to punch me constantly?" Tom shot Josh an angry look. The planchette was already moving.

"Ask Tom," it was written.

Tom was the first to speak up. "Well this is more absurd."

The board was spelled "Dad."

Chris and Josh were looking at each other in awe, confused. They both agreed they were to Tom. In the meantime, Tom had broken into sweat. His eyebrows furrowed, as his skin was red.

The board wrote "Dad" twice more. The third time it happened, Tom leapt up and left the room, crying. This it was the first occasion that the other boys had witnessed Tom crying. It was not until a few days when they found out that Tom had a father who was abusive. Tom did not inform anyone about this information before but the Ouija board was aware.

9: A Life-Changing mistake

The story's narrator tells us that they "were five ladies"; Selena, Martha and Selena's sister Jasmine and a mutual friend named Emma. One day they decided to host an over-night party at the home of the narrator. Her parents had left for the night, and they would not return until into the following day. When the clock struck 7.30 all of the family had arrived at the home.

The fun continued. Martha was the first to arrive. When her turn came, she was carrying the Ouija board. The person who was narrating was intrigued. "Why take this board in with you?" She asked. Martha responded, "Well, we must bring them to our celebration as well." Girls had a great time up to 12 am. After 12 am the girls focused their attention on playing on the Ouija board.

It was a series of normal rituals, lighting candles, and everything. Selena was able to get things moving.

"Is there anyone there who would like to talk to us?"

There was no response by the Board.

Selena was again astonished. "Come to us; don't delay in talking with us!"

There was still no response.

After making requests for 21 requests, they were dissatisfied with the inactive board. They focused their attention on an on-screen TV show. Because the girls had spent in the house of the narrator and decided to change their clothes. When Martha was the next to change to go to the bathroom. Then, she started screaming. The girls jumped up to look around. Martha stated, "Just now, I observed myself walking through the bathroom." At first they thought that they were trying to make them feel scared. However, she pointed out an injury on her arm, which she was able to clearly have not created by herself.

The girls chose to bring back their Ouija board. Narrator played medium this time around.

"Is there anyone in the area?"

The board read "Yes."

"Who is your real name?" Selena asked.

The board was spelled "D."

Jasmine made a statement. "D who?"

The board was spelled "Death."

Martha was the first to speak up. "What do you want us to do?"

The board said "Blood and Your flesh."

The girls attempted to get from the house, but after trying to unlock the door, discovered that it was tightly shut. They began screaming. A supernatural force pulled Selena over the ceiling and Martha with the help of the narration, had to pull her back down. Martha was in a rage.

"Why why don't you be quiet?"

The Ouija board's reply was "Your screaming just makes me stronger."

Chapter 9: The Collection Of Short Ouija Board Horror Stories

The collection of brief Ouija horror stories that are discussed here are more suited to contemplation and deep reflection:

10, The Handprint Horror

The narrator is a woman named Katherine has kept her Ouija account brief and clear:

"When I was just a child," she says, "I was able to try playing with the Ouija board. At the time I was a religious skeptical. When everyone else who was around me believed in the supernatural I would ridicule those who believed in spirits. For my mind, that was an unsubstantiated fable.

But, this time it was I was lucky that the Ouija board was directly in my face. I decided it shouldn't be too bad to play around with it. I asked the board to perform increasingly physical actions. The planchette remained stationary for the entire time.

I went from simple requests, like having the boards tap me on my shoulder to requesting blows. Suddenly, I felt my back sting. The pain was intense and abrupt. I removed my clothing and examined my back using a mirror. my back. There were three marks from my hand on my back. The region was puffy and red as like I'd just had a hard slap."

11. Scary Shadows

Michelle Castillo-Rodriguez relates an experience that was interesting.

The brother of her friend brought the Ouija board home where they played. Then everything went off. The entire family was witnessing marbles and pennies hurled across the hallway, even when they were unable to know who was responsible for the throwing. The lights would turn in and out.

The mother of the boy was working on gardening when she saw an animal. As she sat up straight, she yelled to the dog to move close to her. The dog's face suddenly changed, and then was the look of an old man's face. the woman was terrified. The situation got so bad that the family was forced to seek out the priest to have an exorcism. Even to this day they still witness shadows that trail them all over the home.

Twelve: An Unnerving Whisper

The story's narrator is Josie.

Josie states that for several months, she was involved in what she described as "harmless supernatural phenomenon." After several months of this she decided to purchase an Ouija board to play at home. She began playing it and the planchette subsequently began making figures eights with the Ouija board.

Josie claims she was aware that this was a no-noand that she knew that the appearance of figures of eights appearing on her board was a sign that the board was in contact with a demon who was restless. She promptly put the board away and waited months before touching it again.

When she finally got the sleeve, she inquired whether anyone was there and, If so what was the location of the spirit. Josie states that her vision became blurred. Josie saw the head of her snapping in two and an ear-splitting voice whispering in her ear "I am there together with you."

13: A Bizarre Blackout

Ashley claims she was just 18 when she had an experience using the Ouija board. Her grandmother asked her utilize the board to connect with her uncle, who died when she was born. She did as she was instructed and played with the Ouija to summon the spirit of the spirit of her uncle.

At first, everything was fine. As time went on Ashley's "uncle" was going through an unusual attitude shift. He became a little more edgy and overbearing. After several days the spirit finally admitted that Ashley's uncle was not the one it claimed to be. The spirit however stated that it was her uncle, and was going to be there to her next.

Ashley claims that she was black for about a minute , and she woke up to find that, when she got back her senses, her head was spinning and every light bulb in the room was lit. Ashley never played on the board again.

14. Crayon Catastrophe!

Kristin states that on a hot summer day, she along with her friends, playing on the Ouija board, came across the spirit of Joe. The other peers were skeptical. They continued to push her to prove that the spirits were real. The board was asked to establish the validity of her spirit. The planchette moved, and the board instructed the group to stand up and head to Kristin's bedroom. Naturally, they rushed up the steps.

When they entered the room, they discovered the crayons tossed over and scattered over the floor. One notebook was opened and inside was JOE wrote with crayons. Kristin states that her friends offered some suggestions to her. They suggested she cut the table "into tiny pieces to break it up." She was shocked enough to take their suggestion and then break it.

15 The Old Friend

Patti Viscardi says when her son was in fourth grade, one day at recess, he and classmates were playing with an Ouija board. The boy told her they had spoken to spirits of a 13-year-old boy who claimed to be alive during the Civil War. The son of Patti's returned to her home and shared the tale.

The first time, she paid not much notice of the story. She was puzzled that the school allowed students to play an Ouija board in recess. But she didn't do any announcement about the matter. A few days later her son returned back to tell her that they had been connected to the spirit.

The spirit had said to them that it believed it was an excellent idea for them to be part of it, and it wanted everyone to be friends. Patti was fed up of the whole situation. She rang the school , and according to her own words "had to be a bad mom and remove the board from the school."

16. The Mystery of the Haunted Theatre

Tina Lagerquist gives an interesting account. She claims that at one time in her life, she was employed at what she describes as a "haunted theater." Tina says that one day she and her colleagues decided that it was a good idea to utilize the theatre's board. Tina however, says that the entire meeting was as bizarre as you can get.

Spirits were constantly getting into each other's way, and a total of nine names were spotted in the game board. One of them recognized itself as RD and repeatedly pleaded with the RD to get out. It moved the planchette with a series of figures eights. Tina claims that by the time she quit working at the theater there were many strange happenings in the theatre.

Chapter 10: Celebrity Ouija Board Account Over The Years

While regular civilians have had plenty of Ouija board experiences Celebrities have their fair share of tales to share. This chapter will explore a variety of stories about Ouija board experiences. Ouija board, and also the impact it brought to the lives of celebrities.

17 Sylvia Platth: 17

Sylvia Plath is the author of "Dialogue over an Ouija board," a book she wrote in 1957. It doesn't require skilled mind to realize that the story is about what's known as the Ouija board. Incredibly enthralled by this particular Ouija was she that she even followed the book with a poem on the similar phenomenon.

18, John G Fuller

When Eastern Airlines Flight 401 plummeted into in the Florida Everglades in the year 1972, John G Fuller wrote an article about the incident. He titled the book "The Ghosts from Flight 401."

Eastern Airlines employees Eastern Airlines kept reporting that they saw ghosts of both the pilot as well as the co-pilot of the plane that crashed in the vicinity of the headquarters of the company. They also claimed that they saw ghosts of ten flight attendants who perished after the plane crashed onto other aircrafts.

The hypothesis was that ghosts had a difficult time getting to rest while leaving those who live to themselves because the company who owned the plane snatched out the parts of the ruined plane and put them to use to construct the sole Lockheed plane. Fuller equipped himself with a spirit board , and began to make contact with the spirits in order to collect information to write his book.

19: Poet James Merrill

Even Pulitzer award winners are not immune to encounters in Ouija boards. Ouija board. Poetry writer James Merrill extensively used the Ouija board in his work , including the widely popular "The change of the light in Sandover," a 560 page epic piece. The poem was a message from Archangel Michael his self.

20. Alice Cooper

For starters, Alice Cooper was a male, not a female. He once claimed that the name he chose for his stage came due to his continued utilization of the Ouija board. Before he was given the stage name Alice Cooper, he was Vincent Furnier.

Vincent was able to consult his Ouija board and it informed Vincent that he was Reincarnation of the witch Alice Cooper, a witch who lived in the 17th century. Then he adopted the name of Alice Cooper as his own.

21. Emily Grant Hutchings

The source of among the more well-known applications of the Ouija is given to Emily Grant Hutchings in 1917. She published a book entitled Jap Herron and claimed none other than Mark Twain had dictated it through an Ouija board that she had.

Although some people agreed with her, or at the very least took her story at an unbiased level, the critics had no interest in it, however. They said that the book was a terrible writing that it was impossible that Mr. Twain dead, ou not written the book. It is possible to look the book online if you want to have the pleasure of reading.

22: Pearl Curran

Piss Pearl Curran gained quite the fame due to her Ouija written works. Curran claims that through Ouija, or the Ouija board she wrote the book along with a puritan, called Patience Worth.

Patience Worth, it seems was a prolific writer and published numerous novels as well as a variety of poems prior to Curran's passing in 1937. Patience was a wonderful person. She was generous enough to notify Pearl Curran of her imminent death prior to her death.

22: William Butler Yeats

This person did not utilize a board for himself. He took the advantage of wife's abilities in spiritualism. She was an adept medium. He utilized his wife's channeling abilities to create "A Vision" by using her auto-writing.

The one difference between this method and the use of an Ouija board is that, rather than writing cryptic messages on a board, automated writing is a result of a spirit passing through the hands of the medium and writing notes.

23: Bill Wilson

The book contains an in-depth description of the tale. This book deserves a mention, however. The reason is that Bill Wilson succeeded at dropping an alcohol addiction that was bad. He then followed this victory by acquiring a severe Ouija addiction.

He established the Spook Room inside his home and would make contact with spirits who helped him overcome an addiction to alcohol. One of the spirits, which you might have seen here was a spirit from the 15th century monk known as Boniface.

24: Italian Prime Minister Romano Prodi

There aren't likely to be many politicians who admit to using Ouija boards. Ouija board. In addition the former Italian Premier Romano Prodi is unlike most prime ministers.

Romano Prodi stood tall and under oath, admitted his reason for being certain he knew the exact spot where the Red Brigades had held the former Prime Minister Aldo captive was because of what the Ouija board had informed him.

The judge was interested in knowing more about the matter, and pressed on. "Who did it was who has been revealing that this?" Prodi let on that it was the spirit of Giorgio La Pira, the former Florence mayor who died in the year before.

That he did this under oath suggests that we should be sure to take his words seriously. However, a significant portion of people believe that Romano Prodi was merely throwing the smokescreen to disguise the truth behind his claims.

25: Jane Roberts

Jane Roberts initially contacted 'Seth Seth' via her Ouija board. She says Seth as "an energy essence of the personality that has ceased to exist in the physical universe in the way we perceive it." The book "Seth Speaks" she claims, is it's explanation for "the phenomena known as reality in the way that Seth was able to process it." It is possible to get that book and take a look.

26: G.K. Chesterton

In his teens, G.K. Chesterton avidly played with to play the Ouija board. In the year the year 1893 Chesterton was going through what was described by him as "a period of doubt and depression." In this turbulent time, Chesterton turned to Ouija and this was the beginning of his interest in the mysterious.

27: George Noory

On July 25th, 2007 was an incident of a singular nature that put George Noory right at the in the middle. In an episode of Coast-to-Coast AM, a paranormal radio program the host, Mr. Noory tried to demonstrate the live Ouija experiment. Be aware that this was national radio. A guest was particularly critical, and took every opportunity to rescind the show.

After that, a series of bizarre events started to happen at the radio show's headquarters. In this moment, the guest shared a near-death incident which he once had due to using the Ouija board. Noory when he heard the story, decided to stop the experiment.

Chapter 11: Decoding The Different Possession Accounts And Other Similar Patterns

You may have observed while reading the numerous, often horrifying Ouija board stories in the guide below, you might have noticed that the items are commonplace in Ouija account stories. This chapter will guide you through the horror stories in this book, and try to clarify the events with the help of various sources.

Preamble

The church's view regarding the Ouija board issue because it makes lots from its own without any secular mediums supporting it. You should have realized that there is a religious component to using the Ouija board, and that the Ouija is more than an entertainment device. Some are losing their lives as well as their sanity. They've lost a lot of hours of playing using playing with the Ouija board.

This chapter will take through the demonic possession, and try to explain why things transpired the way they did. It will explain the reasons presented in an approach that will help you understand why you should stay clear of the Ouija board, if you've not taken one yet or know what you can take if you're in trouble. The chapter will focus on a few instances and then break them down into the various aspects of them.

Many thousands of people have used thousands of people have used the Ouija board to try to connect with spiritual beings. The short quick wit here and go through diverse stories and reports, the Ouija board can be extremely hazardous. Like seances and automated writing, the reason for the Ouija board to be extremely dangerous isn't due to the involvement of spirits and repulsion, but rather because there is no way to determine what spirits you'll talk to after you begin playing with the Ouija board.

You might be successful in finding and releasing the spirit you prefer (most people accomplish this, anyway) however, there's always the possibility that another spirit may enter your world.

To coin a phrase you are familiar with, there's not a "firewall" to protect you from unwanted elements. This is the reason that makes the board dangerous to be used. The primary reason people choose to use the Ouija board isn't an urgent need to talk to spirits - just curiosity. However, be aware that using the Ouija board can be typically negative soon after the first time you use it.

The preceding text has explained that the reason that this type of board is dangerous is the lack of a "firewall" that can keep evil spirits from entering. Check out the "David is upset" story. Although it was wise to Ralph Gold to break contact with the spirit who was rogue right away however, the claim that his wisdom might have convinced him not to make use of the board is a valid argument.

In the Search for New Ground: Newbie's Their Exposure to the Spirits of Harm

Another reason that one of the reasons that the Ouija board is extremely dangerous is that the majority of people who use it are ignorant of the risks that could be in store for them. It's like giving a child an instrument for them to use. A toddler who has grown accustomed to sucking on things to fill his time, could attempt to put the blade into his mouth. In the end, it's so shiny and bizarre isn't it? Whatever he decides in using the knife you can bet that when he has enough time, he'll end up hurting himself. The scalpel in this case can be described as the Ouija board, and the youngster represents the majority of people who utilize it or try to make use of it.

A Managed Situation

Controlled situations occur in situations where you intend to perform the Ouija and you are able to are psychic, medium, or clairvoyant present , so that he can detect any dangers and help you avoid the dangers. But, even in this situation there is no security.

The spirits are still able to "make moves behind" and appear as different friendly spirits. In addition, psychic defenses are as nonchalant as they come. the medium is unable to fight the spirit masquerading as him All the medium can do is stop the communication. If he's lucky, it will happen before doing any serious damage.

So, the idea of a "controlled scenario" is not really a reality. When you play Ouija boards, it is not a controlled situation. Ouija board, it's an open space with spirits emerging from the woodwork to play whatever they like.

The Spirits

It is important to understand that the majority of spirits that are contacted via the board are those who reside in "the the lower plane of astral." The spirits that are contacted are, therefore, are often disturbed or confused or have perhaps met their deaths with a violent or sudden manner. They could have passed away in the past, but not before they had time.

This means that an endless amount of negative, violent potential dangers are available to anyone who uses the board. Consider the scenario that is "David," for instance. In many cases, multiple spirits attempt to break through simultaneously and attempt to fool the audience. For this reason, the illustration of "David" is sufficient.

The story of the Robert Stamper family: A Analysis and Explanation

Most of the time, when you're just beginning, it's mostly entertainment and playing. It can even be friendly, with introductions were made (This is Seth or this is Seth, etc.) Although you're making an efforts to invoke the spirits the spirits appear to have taken a page from the book of vampires of behavior.

The spirit cannot "come into" unless you allow it to. You can invite the spirit into your home through asking it to provide PHYSICAL evidence that it exists. It could be, "If you really are an entity then why don't you take away the shoe rack, or even put on this light for me, okay?" Now, what you've done is easy: you've successfully opened the doorway and allowed the spirit in your physical realm.

The spirit, in itself does not have the ability to establish its will on the physical world until you give the power. However, the power can only be used in one direction. You are able to decide the moment it enters your physical realm however it isn't your decision to decide the time it will go away. The potential for future problems to arise in particular when you experience fear of spirit and want to dispel it away.

Notice how the spirit only gets unleashed once you "open the door" by giving it instructions to do something physical. Be aware of the difference in activities from the spirit while it was at peace to introduce itself in a harmless manner and expressing itself, it unleashed its evil when granted permission to express it physically.

Another fact: even the gentle spirits are scams. They're usually identical and are evil, and prone to harm you. The reason they seem to be friendly is that they intend to gain access to you in order to grant them access to the world around you which they are unable to do by themselves. If you are doing this, your friendliness tends to fade quickly. There are exceptions, and some spirits might continue to maintain the act of friendship for longer, however the final result is always the same.

Confessions of a Spiritual experimenter' (Featuring Richard)

It's possible that it's too early, in the sense that the book is concerned there is a pattern evident that the spirits tend to be drawn towards dark and evil. What you will get when you use your Ouija board: spirits of darkness who are most likely to destroy your life, rather than making it better as you might have wanted. Beware of the lies, this is the usual pattern throughout the world.

Preamble

In the case of the Ouija board debate is concerned there is a split between two groups. The first is known as the anti-Ouija group, and the law enacted by this group is that the Ouija board is a sinister device that should not be touched.

Then , we will are in the middle of the camp. It will be the Parker brothers the camp of the Parker brothers. The Parker brothers' camp is steadfast in their conviction in the idea that an Ouija board, once you take it off to its bare bones, is just a game that provides "better insights into your own."

Who's telling the truth? If you're not acquainted of the reality that Parker brothers produce Ouija boards (and earn million of dollars) Continue reading and let the reader decide. This book will provide an argument that is fair as well as a few examples that are valid.

1st Argument 1st Argument Jane Roberts and Seth Story

Jane's Ouija account is identical to Pearl Curran's account that was wiped out in

1913 and the account related to Stewart Edward White and his wife in 1919. Both occurred several years prior to Jane's account.

Based on the White's account, Betty White was the person who entered the trance, and through it she communicated with spirits through the Ouija Board. The couple studied for 17 years the way that Betty communicated with a group of discarnate creatures who were known as "the invisibility of the invisibles."

After making her first contact with an Ouija board Betty was able to begin using automatic writing . Later, she would proceed to trance mediumship. As was the case with Jane The spirits would use the vocal chords of Betty. It is clear out that the spirits are using you as a means to force any will in the physical realm. The main phrases here are Use YOU.

2nd Argument The Lie Will Never Stop

This is the main argument Christians and a large part of mediums make in support of Ouija is a dangerous game. Ouija is extremely risky and those who promote it as an innocent game are in fact lying to you. This is what they claim:

Be assured that the lies continues to circulate. The truth is that you should believe in Ouija board as a mere Ouija board as just a game for entertainment. It is a shame not believing in the supernatural is real and the Ouija board as a gateway to it. The thing is it is that Ouija boards are not a spiritual device. Ouija board can be described as a religious device that is advertised as a game with questions that are posed and answers are interpreted as if they were divine: This is the simple truth.

3rd Argument 3rd Argument Passport to Hell Story (The Sun)

Read the previous paragraphs. The first part claims that the majority of people who utilize this Ouija board for summoning spirits, are novices who don't know more about it. For them, it's nothing just a game, and the whole summoning process is a long humorous joke.

They don't realize that many mediums themselves stay clear of the board, citing "spiritual weight" that the board can bring because it is too unstable."

The signs of naivete are obvious. Take note of how John and Gloria employ words such like "joke," "accident," "play," etc. An experienced medium would have ended the channeling between the spirits as fast as he possibly could have done before any harm was done. You might also have seen how the spirit asked John if it was possible to visit them and John agreed. Go back to the tale and watch how it goes down after John unlocks the gate for the spirit.

Although the Ouija board is still very popular and is which is commercially sold as an "game" (today being sold through The Parker brothers) it is imperative to consider that there must be a motive that it has come under numerous attacks from those who are those who oppose the occult. There has to be a reason behind why people who belong to the occult world view Ouija boards in the occult as "unsafe." The majority of the spirits you summon are either in deep trouble or are in deep trouble. This is the way they operate.

Fourth Argument: A Ghost that simply refuses to go away

The book has already addressed the fact that spirits are extremely resistant to leave. For maximum impact you must remember this small piece of wisdom for the record: even though you have the ability to call spirits from its dwelling to enter the physical world but it isn't in your control to choose the moment it returns. You may call it back to your own life, but letting it off is difficult.

Look at the way the story unfolds. When you bring the spirit of your world and give it the power to manifest itself physically. Resistance is also a method of expression. An Christian writer speaks of "giving you the right of the Spirit to govern your existence." This is a good idea.

Let's say, for example that a magistrate judge rule for your spouse who divorced you receiving full custody of the child and orders the child to be paid child support on an annual basis. It is impossible to argue with this. If you do, you are fighting the legal system, which can only land you into serious trouble.

Of of course, Ouija board spirits are not subject to such strict control as the law. If you've granted the spirit the the power to oppose your will and influence specific aspects of your existence, how can you think it would be able to thwart the wishes of its spirit to affect your life simply because you have told it to? Be careful before you try Ouija boards. Ouija board.

When we discussed the tale of the spirit who would not go away, have noticed that there was not a mention about the ghost that he summoned that was haunting his lover. Take a look at the rule of 51 that is not actually a rule, but when applied in this case. One more important issue to consider is Martin's conviction that a person of good will could never be so smug.

This is the truth Many mediums claim to believe in the absence of any risk of losing a job "good" as well as "bad" spirits don't exist. The legendary spiritual leader Nicky Cruz, a man who was once the leader of"the "Mau-Mau," a vicious street gang in New York, put it the best way.

He claimed that evil and good spirits are not real. Every spirit is evil, in reality, they are not the spirits you think of them. They are mere demons who disguise themselves as something else. Once you die and your spirit departs the body, it ceases to have any power to affect the earth's natural environment as well as "come to return." Nicky Cruz would knowthat his parents were shamans, who with the assistance from "good" spirits helped many people get rid of negative spirits.

The best advice for Martin who is the youth, would be to seek out a man of cloth with expertise in exorcism. However, even then, it's not always clear whether the spirits will depart. It is best to imagine that the damage may have already taken place (Martin mentions his right eye becoming uncontrollably twitchy in addition to other pains). The most effective advice is to avoid playing with the board initially since you can be sure that what you invoke will certainly cause harm to you. But, there's always the chance that something life-altering might occur.

One of the reasons that people who are curious tell us is that despite the fact that they play playing with an Ouija board and invoke bad spirits, their faith shields them from danger. It's unfortunate that the majority of those who offer such arguments are Christians who adhere to an ancient religion that is so good and legitimate, yet it doesn't provide any guidelines that you must follow.

Whatever way your float is in the realm of religion it is important to realize it's a foolish argument. If you're a Christian who has considered following such a premise and you are a Christian, the Bible declares, "...for whoever engages in spiritism, God will turn his back toward him." In other words, if you consider yourself to be a Christian and believe in God and the Lord God turns his face away from you, your security is certainly gone, isn't it? Some people think that if they become in a state of possessedness, they can simply remove the spirit and get rid of it. Reread the stories time, and you'll realize that when it comes to Ouija boards, there's anything simple or easy.

If it's unclear, trying to ward off the spirit, praying to the name of Jesus or participating in any other spiritual practice to deter spirits doesn't mean that you will get the results you desire. In reality 99 percent of the time the spirit will mount an energetic and sometimes terrifying resistance.

The spirit will always be within you, you'll be the first to be injured. Check out some exorcism video clips on the internet e.g. YouTube and notice how dishonest the unfortunate victims are; the pain is evident for you to be able to see.

Take a look at how Martin's influence over the spirit is still limited. Martin has a rule that it should not speak to him again, but there must be one exception. This will put quite a weight on his head; Knowing that in the coming years, it will be the time that Spirit will talk to him once more - and the spirit will be completely out of control over it at all.

What you will get when you use Ouija boards. Ouija board. It lets you sell your control of your own internal affairs for a spirit that is foreign and receive nothing in return.

In this chapter, we have already discussed the fact that "good" spirits don't exist. It has clarified to you that in the beginning , when the doorway is closed and the spirit is unable to find a method of manifesting physically The spirit appears welcoming.

It is important to note that it insists that you ask questions. If you ask a question you ask it to establish its legitimacy. It opens that access to the physical world. Once this is done, the spirit eventually gets tired of the game and begins to take over more. This is the way it is always.

Martin does everything according to the rules, but the spirit is refusing to go away. If it was as easy as a prayer to God and reciting the name of God, this story could be over sooner than it did. Be aware that once you've opened the gate into the spiritual realm, it's really difficult to push it to go back.

Martin is a fervent Christian. But his religious beliefs have so not been able to eliminate the spirit. As a person who is religious when you fall asleep and call a spirit on your Ouija board, it's likely for the spirits to annoy you for the rest of your life.

Do the Demons On The Ouija Board Discriminate Or Give preference to certain groups?

It is obvious like a day to know that this isn't the scenario. The Ouija board spirits employ the same strategy for everyone. As we've observed that they will provide you with an amiable tone. Once you accept the offer and "open the door," the darkness starts. Even the young are not left out.

The point in Cindy's story:

See how the spirit appears as her friend from long ago Jake and lures her in, so that she is closer as time passes. However, the pattern is generally similar. The spirit usually loses the desire to play and start showing its true colours as days pass. Watch how demons usually leave an opportunity to attack at the end of the game.

The tale that follows the story of three brothers is an excellent idea in the event of:

The spirit of the Ouija board is a delicate topic. Take a take a look at the effectiveness of the way it communicates. "Dad" has the potential to be just as blunt as it gets yet it is able to convey maximum impact.

The lesson to be learned here is Ouija board demons are not able to provide any special treatment. No matter if you're a kid or a young adult or an older man, regardless of whether you're either a male or female all things are equal. If you believe that you'll get any kind of a pass due on your age, or gender, consider changing your mind. What you undergo, and if you believe that the stories here can be a guideline they will be like any others we've seen.

Note This is the Abstract Rule of 51

Do the spirits on Ouija boards harm people who use them? Ouija board harm all who utilizes the Ouija board?

Chapter 12: Ouija And Its Haunting Powers

The Ouija is composed of a level board, on which are printed the letters from the set of letters along with a few numbers, accentuation marks, as well as two wordings "yes" or "no". The participants continue to put their fingers gently on a pointer. The board is then, apparently without cognizant effects of their actions, is illuminated by a series of messages.

A lot of users who use the Ouija board frequently view this as a way to get people interested in gatherings or other social gatherings and events, but without fully comprehending the certain risks, of which there are a variety of. The Ouija board is a possibility and often is effective as well, and there are a lot of messages received could originate coming from "the different side". However, a few of these connections are with beings that reside within the lowest areas of the Astral

Planes, whose objectives are usually much lower than fair.

As previously mentioned the creatures and people living in the smallest Astral realms behave so because of their dull hostile and here and there violent lives they had during their time on Earth and, correspondingly, live at these similarly lower energy level of vibrancy. The danger to this is that, the lower on the Astral plane that the creature is the easier it will be to get to the physical world via the Ouija load, because of the internal relative densities as well as the lower vibrations relative to the Ether.

The creatures from Lower Astral universes can as frequently as possible take pleasure in claiming that they are Angels, Archangels, well recognized individuals, or God while others be unaffected in claiming to be dead people, as Ouija board participants. At different times, these lower astral creatures can use obscenities, snark and generally speaking in a awful dialects. What is the reason the lower astral creatures go their language in this manner?

In addition to the fact that this is often the case of these creatures and therefore the reason they are in lower Astral universes at all and their devastation is frequently extended to an amazing degree because of their physical limitations. are unable to never physically experience what they enjoyed at one time and were frequently squandered to the extent that they're physically alive, such as the aforementioned leniency in wrongdoing recklessness, violence, drunkenness as well as excessive medication use, and sex that is not arousing any evidence of love, appreciation or excitement. If they had any acceptable limit of affection, love for musings, or any other positive qualities and qualities, they wouldn't be in the position they are in. If they were able to ask for help to rid their misery This assistance could be offered by the more evolved internal creatures, if they were suitable.

Mediums who have met creatures that reside at these astral levels often report hearing negative, oppressive, and nasty voices. These are those same creatures who are often encountered through the use of Ouija sheets. Unfortunately, due to the fact that those who use the Ouija board on the Ouija board are usually looking for and hoping for genuine contacts with inner levels of Spirits They will often be sucked in by the deceitful actions of the lower astral creatures.

Lower Astral creatures don't like living in their boring universes they will always grab every opportunity to gain control of the physical body within the physical world. This can easily lead to the full control of the body, which can cause many possible terrifying issues, but not limited to extremely grave mental problems. The person who is influenced person may alter drastically and, for the worse. The primary solution to this kind of situation, which is a matter of ownership is to cleanse the entity of the person who is being influenced. This could seem quite emotional following what started as a harmless, fun-filled gathering however it could occur, and it does happen, it is essential that everyone Ouija board users should be aware of the dangers prior to using an Ouija board for any kind of gathering bizarre.

The Ouija board should always be considered to be an extremely risky device and should be avoided from the inside and outside. Anyone who is tempted to ignore these dangers should at all times be aware of the ways of people who are liable to be impacted and also what their actual thoughts are often. For instance, any being that claims that they are a deceased loved one should be investigated by asking questions to which only family members would know the answer. This same principle is applicable to any creature who claim that they are Angels, Archangels or wellfamous people. These creatures in reality have no knowledge of Angels, Archangels or the famous people they claim as being, but could effectively be removed. Furthermore, it's essential to remember that this type of behavior is an explanation for why the creatures reside in the lowest part of the astral worlds regardless of their circumstances. They generally aren't should be relied upon without a doubt unless examined by a professional who understands the risks.

Stoker Hunt an individual who did studies into the consequences that can result through the use of for the Ouija board, described an instance of the correspondence that people can be created when people encounter substances in the low level of the astral worlds. He explained:

"The intruder focuses on weak points of the victim's character, in the case of vanity and lusty, pleas to vanity are used. "I need your help," the seducer might claim, 'only you are able to help me'. The person is malicious and will not shy away from lying, misrepresenting it (usually as a family member) and even flatter. It's best for the invader to be sure that the victim is in a lonely place in isolation, sick and lonely. If it is necessary, the invader is able to terrorize its victimby appearing in terrifying form, provoking bizarre visions, and inciting an occult activity, and appearing as objects from nowhere and delivering negative or sad information, levating objects and even levitating the victim. These and many other things could happen not to achieve a goal among themselves, but rather as an opportunity to gain total possession".

It should be obvious that at this point, the Ouija board could be an dangerous instrument to be certain, especially for those who do not know the full implications. Doctor. Carl Wickland, an American specialist, wrote his superb take at the issue of emotional illness in his book "Thirty Years of the dead" in 1924. Within the book he advises:

"The complex issue of alienation and mental confusion resulting from mindless psychic explorations was initially brought to my attention through the stories of a few individuals whose seemingly innocent exercises using computer-generated compositions and the Ouija board triggered an uncontrollable mania that commitment to refuges was needed. A variety of ill-fated outcomes that resulted from the use of the likely innocent Ouija board came to my attention and my thoughts pushed me to study psychic phenomena to find a possible explanation of these strange incidents".

These are just a handful of possible outcomes that can be derived from using this Ouija board. It is important to make explicit that not all communications through using the Ouija board are fraudulent There have also been several positive, long-term conversations where it's been possible to communicate with good-natured and amiable inward-level Astral creatures. One of the most significant instances was the one from Pearl Curran who utilized an Ouija board along with her friend on the 12th of July, 1912. After a period of time of testing she began to receive communications of Patience Worth, a Spirit entity who claimed that she was born by 1649, at Dorsetshire, England. Between 1912 and 1919 she wrote 5 million words across the board, which included sayings and lyrics, books of full length as well as moral stories or short story. Her total works comprised the pages of twenty nine volumes bound and 4375 pages that were single separated. The works comprised five books that were full length which included the best of them all "The The Sorry Tale" which is a 300,000-word account of the natural life of Jesus which was read in the New York Times on July 8, 1917. They wrote: "This long and perplexing account about Jewish as well as Roman life in the time of Christ is written using the exactness and precision of an experienced hand. It's an amazing book, an enchanting and prestigious book". Persistence Worth was awarded numerous distinctions and awards throughout the years, for a vast variety of abstract works.

Another well-known Spiritual element that first appeared through the Ouija board was named "Seth" and first appeared at the time Jane Roberts and her spouse first began using an Ouija board as part of the year 1963. The essence in the end showed itself to be Frank Withers who passed on in 1942, following his final physical activity as an English teacher. He was fond of being known as "Seth" and stated his main goal of helping people understand themselves and their surroundings more clearly.

In the course of Jane Roberts, Seth directed several highly rated books that dealt with the ways of reality, resurrection astral travel, dreams , and the ways of God. Seth also gave a series of logical lectures on the process of contemplation and physical discernment. Seth was also prepared to study diseases, visualize the structure and rooms that were distances away. He also even appear as a phantom within light-colored settings.

There have been a myriad of successful uses that made use of the Ouija board which turned out to be of immense value to the persons involved as well as, every now and then like Seth for all mankind. This shouldn't be considered a valid reason in itself to validate the inherent dangers of using Ouija boards. Ouija board. James Merrill, a Pulitzer winner, relates his Ouija board experiences when he wrote "The changing light in Sandover" during 1982. His enthralling experiences, which included visions, major changes, the development of habitations that are effective, and more vital and positive ones are captured in the song. In the following thirty years, however, the author no longer advises people to using the Ouija board due to the fact that "one cannot predict how vulnerable an individual is".

In terms of equalization, the use of an Ouija board must be completely discouraged. Due to how this instrument functions, it is a lot more likely to attract violent low-level astral entities than sane or helpful creatures of the internal level. People who draw in creatures of lower levels are at a higher probability of suffering or a genuine emotional illness and both could be difficult to conquer using the current methods of restorative therapy. The best solution to such an extreme situation, which includes among dimensional strengths is an expulsion performed by an experienced and highly skilled professional which there aren't too many in our current society.

The most effective method, then, is to resist any such threats completely, but in the event you ever feel the need to make use of it to reach the spirits of the dead, please use it according to the rules!

Chapter 13: Skepticism About Talking Boards

There appears to have been a lot of skeptical science in the current era of modern technology with regards the existence of talking-boards.

According to some famous scientists, there is an incredibly more rational explanation for these "messages" from the past, and they're unchangeably found in a rational world.

The Ouija board relies on what people refer to as the Idomotor Impact that refers to the impact that subliminal and nuanced thoughts can have on the development of muscles. The concept is that you cannot stop your muscles from fully moving and that subliminal thoughts could have an impact on the subtle movements of those muscles, regardless of when you think you're not moving.

In reflexive responses to suffering the body in certain instances responds to thoughts by itself, without the person consciously taking a step. For instance, tears are caused by the body in unintended ways as a response to the sensation of sadness.

Due to this Ouija boards, this effect causes the user to determine where the marker is moving, regardless of whether the person is aware of it or not.

A tendency to want to witness anything "unusual" or "spooky" occur or be in a rush to talk to a lost or loved one has an effect on the impact as well. In this case, your hand will move in the right direction and again the client may not be aware of it.

A study to prove this effect is easy. Connect a thin piece of string onto a metal bolt, or some other thing that is tiny and usually large. Hold the string in your fingers and the arm in front of it (with an nut hanging through the strings). Now, keep your arm as steady as it is possible to do until you're satisfied that your arm isn't moving. If you begin to imagine the hex nuts moving and then be focused on it, the nut will definitely begin to move regardless of the fact that you do not consider your arm moving.

For those who aren't convinced The reason is that tiny subtle, intuitive movements in your arm, which are influenced by your goals and impact of your ideomotor is being interpreted through the string before being transferred to the hexagonal the nut. If you can think of the mechanism behind this it is possible to be seamlessly linked directly to an Ouija board.

The outcomes of the ideomotor effect can be seen in the following ways in the event that you have to be witness to something or converse with someone who has died These musings of the mind be observed through subtle muscle movements. The development of these muscles is completely controlled by the user, and provides a solid explanation of the reason why people get responses to specific questions.

In essence the natural explanation for a particular event will be more probable than an supernatural explanation. The Ouija board is a fantastic psychological calming device, or a fantastic party trick, but it's not a supernatural experience. We can enjoy the thought of connection it can provide to loved ones that have passed on or spirits. But it is more real to be able to see the reality of what is happening.

It is far more likely that an explanation that is physical, such as the Idomotor Effect which is the main reason Ouija boards can appear creepy. Compare this to the alternative explanation that a ghost travels across the vast realm of the spirit world to take your hands in order that you are able to communicate with spirits that are dead and then the authenticity that is associated with the Ouija board will be shattered.

I believe you could draw some conclusions from this alternative explanation. It is possible that you are not communicating with spirit via a the wooden board however, you are dealing with internal conflicts that need to be resolved. The Ouija board could be helping with this process of resolving conflicts however, it's internal and normal.

Any doubt of this kind is likely to be answered by something like "you're not open" or "it cannot be resolved". A few non-adherents are able to go against the two statements. There is a chance that you are currently having a open-mindedness when you look at confirmation that's coincident with all the things we believe about our world. It is important to be cautious that you accept any idea or theory, or to be so open to the idea that your brain is unable to function. We know that our mental habits may have unintentional effects on the muscle development.

Have ever wondered why scientists tend to steer clear of the supernatural? The issue is that the prior definitions limited the kinds of explanations that scientists can offer and analyze to the most common ones, stating that science cannot ponder the most extraordinary explanations. To comprehend the significance of this think about the bizarre notion that gravity is caused by heavenly dwarfs that are invisible connecting everything in the universe with inexplicably chewing gum. This could or might not be true, but in the traditional definition, science cannot think about that kind of clarification because it's powerful. The definition that was changed in 2005 revision, however allows any kind of clarification, including supernatural and heavenly, to be brought to be incorporated into science, as long as it addresses everyday phenomenon. Based on the updated definition, the elf-based explanation of gravity can be included in science classes! Despite the fact we're laughing about dwarves, this is a legitimate one. A change in definition could have opened up the doors of science classrooms to all seeking to present their ideas of powerful causation to students in schools that are funded by the state and then pass those views to students as legitimate science.

The current science is unable to handle extraterrestrial clarifications, arguing that they're not tested. As the case may be, there's no way to gather evidence that can help us to determine whether or not the clarifications are precise. Contrary to extraordinary clarifications, ordinary clarifications generate specific desires that are able to compare with proofs from the everyday world in order to determine whether the clarification is likely to be precise. For instance, the speed of an object due to gravity increases when the weight of the object increases. This explanation for one aspect of gravitational fascination creates particular desire tests. If the idea was correct that a ball and a larger lead chunk similar in size should to be falling at different rates as the lead ball experiencing greater speeding. This test can be performed and, if we do, we'll discover that the thought (falling at different rates) is not in line with our thoughts, which suggests that the assumption could be incorrect. Now, think about our absurd alternative explanation for gravity. Consider elves contemplating gum. Do they add the same type in gum for a ball as well as lead ball? Would they apply additional high-end Gum to the lead ball so that it falls faster? Who knows what creatures from the other world that are secretly mulling over gum could choose to do?

In spite of the fact that we can't see what happens when we drop ball, two of them could just imagine a way to attribute it to Elf. The most powerful explanations, due to their unique character, cannot be attempted using routines of science. This doesn't mean they're incorrect, they're simply outside the scope of what science can honestly to investigate. Any attempt to alter the way science is thought of to incorporate extraterrestrial explanations may be causing a misconceptions about science's primary objective that is to gather solid information about the world as a perspective of the normal explanation.

Certain scientists have criticised the media for encouraging paranormal beliefs. In a paper (Singer and Benassi 1981) stated that the media could be responsible for a large portion of the widespread belief in paranormal phenomena because the general public is constantly exposed to media, movies documentaries, books and documentaries that endorse paranormal theories, but criticism is absent. [81 Based on Paul Kurtz "In regard to the numerous talk shows that are constantly dealing with paranormal issues the skeptical view is seldom heard. And when it is allowed to be voiced, it is generally sandbagged by the host or by other guests." Kurtz explained the acclaim of belief among the public in the supernatural as an "quasi-religious phenomenon" which is the manifestation of a spiritual inclination to people to believe in a higher real-world reality that isn't accessible by the methods of science. Kurtz described this as the primitive nature of magic thinking. [82]

Terence Hines has written that at a personal level paranormal claims can be considered to be a type of fraud on consumers since they are "being attracted by fraudulent claims to invest their money, often in large amounts--on paranormal beliefs which don't live up to the promises they make" and a blind acceptance of paranormal beliefs can cause harm to society. (Wikipedia).

Afraid of the Unknown and Death Itself

Everybody thinks about death often. However, there are people who are caught up in the subject of death frequently. They are afflicted by the negative effects of the fear of death. Pavel Ponomaryov, a clinician and therapist, as well as Grigory Chausovsky who is a right-hand teacher in the department of physiology in Zaporozhye the national university, talked about this unusual masochist expression and treatment strategies.

"Everybody is worried about death, but people suffering due to thanatophobia worry about the unknown, and"Ponomaryov clarifies.

"As the rule, fear is felt when there is a risk to an individual's life It is also coordinated by the source of threat or saw and thanatophobia appears to pay not much attention to its presence and is always linked to the death."

According to Chausovsky the spread of thanatophobia can be seen throughout the population of cities. "It is triggered by the fear of criminals through media, which creates an our instinctive fear of becoming criminals or terrorists," he says. "Hereditary characteristics also contribute to these fears (20 percent) and, in addition, hormone imbalance, trauma-related situations and so on."

People who are experiencing this anxiety are focused on the trepidation. They may be afraid of riding on the metro with the fear of dying from an attack by terrorists or even flying in an airplane to avoid crushing. They might visit specialists regularly and undergo tests to test the fear of tumor. They are afflicted by the adverse effects of sleeping insufficiently as well as low charisma and unprofessional conduct, such as telling everyone about the reasons to be concerned. Some start drinking or taking drugs.

Sometimes, a dreadful thought regarding death or illness trigger real sicknesses. Psychoses, anxiety disorders and psychosomatic illness are a result of an intense anxiety.

When people aren't equipped to control their condition or controlling their illness They should look for help from a professional. Exercises for the mind can help make sense of life by accepting death. Everybody has to deal with the subject of death. Some are able to handle it on their own Some require expert assistance.

You might be asking at this point "What exactly is Thanatophobia"?

The term "death anxiety" refers to the morbid anxiety, abnormal or perpetual fear of one's death. A definition of the term "death anxiety" is a "feeling of dread, anxiety or a sense of trepidation (anxiety) when one is thinking about death, dying or ceasing to "be"". It's also referred to by the name of the fear of death (fear about death) and is different from necrophobia that is a fear of dying or dead objects or people (i.e. other people who are dying or dead or dying, not necessarily one's own death or death). A lower ego integrity, higher physical ailments, and greater psychological issues can indicate more anxiety over death in older adults.

"The notion of our destruction is like a flash that is ablaze in darkness, which is able to spread its flames over the objects it is about to devour. We should be accustomed to thinking about the light that is shining, as it proclaims nothing that hasn't been planned by everything before. And since death is just as normal as life itself, why should we be scared from it"?

- Louis, chevalier de Jaucourt

Three kinds of anxiety over death:

Tension from passing that is numb

The ruthless tension of passing comes from the fear of being injured. It is the primary and oldest form of death discomfort, with its roots in the early unicellular organic entity's arrangement of diverse resources. Life forms with unicellular receptors that have developed to deal with threats from outside and have self-defense and receptive systems designed to protect themselves from substance physical threat or assault. For humans, this kind of fear is brought on through a myriad of risky situations that put the victim in risk or hinders their life. The injuries could be psychological or physical. Predatory demise nerves are the basis for the individual's plethora of assets and can lead to combat or flight, dynamism efforts to combat the threat or to escape from the danger.

Nervousness about predators or predation

Predation , also known as predator passing nervousness is a kind of death tension that arises from an individual who is physically or intentionally hurting another. This kind of death anxiety is often accompanied by indifference to guilt. This guilt, in turn, encourages and supports a variety of choices and actions made that cause harm to other people.

Existential demise uneasiness

The feeling of being in a state of existential death is the crucial learning and the awareness that the normal course of life has to come to an end. It is believed that existence tension that passes is linked to dialect. In other words dialect has created the foundation for this kind of death anxiety by making changes to the way we behave. It is recognized that existential demise is to be not the most powerful type. There is a reassurance of the distinction between of oneself as well as others, a complete sense of one's own character and the ability to see the future. Humans defend themselves against this type of death apprehension through refusing and this is accomplished through many physical and mental processes, many of which remain unnoticed. While foreswearing that is restricted in use tends to be flexible but its usage is typically expensive and can be costly emotionally.

The consciousness of human mortality began to emerge around 150,000 years ago. Within that to a significant degree limited compass of development time, the human race has developed but one crucial system that they use to control the tensions that this consciousness has generated: disavowal in all its varieties. Therefore, disavowal is essential to the various actions that involve disobeying norms and abuse of limitations and casings, extreme events, roughness that is coordinated with other people, attempts to gain the amount of wealth and influence, and so on. These kinds of interests typically are brought about by an injury that is not a direct cause. taking into consideration that they can cause valuable actions, but usually they trigger activities that both in the short and over time, harmful to oneself and others.

Sigmund Freud was of the opinion that people feel a fear of death, which is known as thanatophobia. Freud believed that this was an excuse for a deeper source of anxiety. There was no demise that people feared because of the fact that from Freud's view, no one is a believer in their specific passing. The uninitiated cannot manage the advancing of time with refutations, and cannot determine the amount of time remaining in one's life. Furthermore, what one is afraid of could not be the end of one's life, in light of the reality that nobody has passed away. People who express fears of death concerns, actually are trying to handle the tense youth conflict which they are unable to handle or express feelings towards. The term Thanatophobia originates with the help of the Greek character of death referred to as Thanatos.

Mohammad Samir Hossain, faculty at Bangabandhu Sheikh Mujib Medical University and Medical College for Women and Hospital was the one who proposed the hypothesis of adjustment and death.

After the declaration these hypotheses two points were proposed. The first portion of the hypotheses suggests that death is not taken as the end of the world. The following section outlines that the eternal human condition is only possible to live an ethically rich lifestyle in a moral stance and materialism balancing.

What do you think are the basis for fear to cling very seriously? You're about to go to take a walk in the wooded areas. amazing, animate sunlight rays through the leaves. Then, suddenly, a diamondback appears right at your feet. You feel something right then and there. Your body is solidified your body, your heart rate goes up and you begin to sweat -- a rapid program of physical reactions. This is the response to apprehension, or more appropriately, fear. After one week, you're walking the same route once more. The sun is shining, you are happy, and there's you haven't encountered a snake that is poisonous. Yet, you're concerned about the possibility of encountering one. The feeling of walking through the forest areas is a stressful one. It's a tense time.

This fundamental remark that occurs in the midst of anxiety and anxiety is an essential part of diagnosing and treating the tension issues, which affect an enormous number of people and result in the most visits made to psychological wellbeing experts each year than any other general categories of psychiatric issues.

However it's the fact that matters is that the line between of nervousness and trepidation can become extremely thin and fluffy. If you have seen the snake at a particular point in the course of your walkand you are at this point the stone could remain in the direction of the snake, and cause anxiety, despite the fact that the snake is disappearing in a mysterious manner. Today, a lot of fear states are like these -- they're caused by certain things such as signs, signs or signposts that are left to be damaged instead of items which are actually dangerous. Following the

September. 11 attacks, for instance, many Americans felt uncomfortable with the sound of low-flying aircrafts.

What happens when things represent dangers? Remember Pavlov's puppy? The moment the ringer called the dog, it was salivating because the chime had already heard as the dog was getting nourished (really the chime wasn't even a Ringer, but it was a ringer regardless). The dog's brain formulated an association to the sound as well as food that the sound would provide, and it was likely to induce salivation as it waited to eat. As the snake case and the September. 11 cases previously mentioned exactly what can happen in extremely dangerous circumstances.

Analysts have a large amount about what happens in the brain whenever jolts of fear become memories that trigger the danger. To make it sound quite simple (however not wrong) the area of the brain known as the amygdala ties together the two incidents, creating an inexplicably oblivious mind to the linkage. The moment that the unidirectional the jolt (the rock or sound from an airplane) is later experienced it will naturally trigger the amygdala as the first incident, creating a sense of apprehension as well as triggering stress tension. The programmatic way of the enactment procedure is similar to how the amygdala performs its function in the absence of conscious mindfulness. We are able to react to risk and after which we acknowledge that peril is there.

Every creature (counting creepy crawlies , worms, but other creatures similar to us) is born with the capacity to identify and react to particular kinds of risks, as well as learn about the things that are associated with risk. In simple terms the capacity to feel trepidation (in the sensation of recognizing and reacting to risks) is very common in all creatures. However the feeling of anxiety is a sign of uncertainty is a different subject. It is based on the ability to predict the future, a limitation that is found in various other species, but that especially prevalent in humans. We can expand our reach into the future like any other animal.

Although nervousness is often characterized by instability, tension in humans is heightened by our capacity to see the future and the place we play in it, including the future that is physically unimaginable. Through our imagination, we can think about the yet to be realized and possibly incomprehensible scenario. This ability to think creatively can lead us to create a fascinating point of interest as we consider ways we can improve our lives however, we could also allow it to work with no benefit and wringing our hands in agony over the outcomes of our actions. The worry over the results is essential to success in overcoming challenges and opportunities. In the end, however we will probably stress more than we need to. This raises the question of how much anxiety and stress are excessive? What can we tell when we've stayed clear between tension and stress to a more serious disorder?

Did you know that many famous people throughout history were consulted by the Ouija many of them were very successful, while some were not so lucky? In the next chapter, we'll be able to discover the stories of successful people and those who were believed to have been led to a certain death.

Chapter 14: Famous People

Consulting Ouija

Talking boards have turned into an iconic piece of pop culture, as shown through their appearances in a variety of movies and books. Their roles in these vary from sly articles to subversive things. The more unusual aspect of talking boards in writing comes from the fact that writers use the board to organize their entire compositions from those who have died.

In the late 1800s, St. Louis housewife Pearl Curran utilized her Ouija board correspondences with a spirit named Patience Worth to share different compositions and lyrics. Pearl claimed that the bulk of her compositions were passed to her in seances which she allowed the rest of society to join in.

Let's first discover what Patience Worth actually was. On a cool, autumn evening that took place in 1919. A crowd of New Yorkers sat in into the living room at the East Side town house to meet a writer called Patience Worth. A shrewd charmer famous for her shrewd mental tricks and quick wit, Patience managed two unique ballads about Russia and the Red Cross in rapid succession, followed by a lyrical song to the supervisor's companion.

Despite the fact that she seemed to take the chips in the moment her words sounded like the ferocity of messages spelled out by printers. The artist Edgar Lee Masters was among the stunned guests. "There there isn't any doubt...she is producing some impressive writing," the writer of Spoon River Anthology told a journalist, but "how she manages to do it, I am not able to tell you." He also wasn't able to describe what Patience looked like, though she was believed to be beautiful and young with her wavy red hair and large eyes made of chestnut. There was no one who actually saw her. She was not genuine. She was an enthusiastic spirit, a fervent soul.

The year 1917 was the time Emily G. Hutchings was a friend to Pearl Curran, accepted she had written to and corresponded with Pearl Curran. She also wrote an article, titled Jap Herron, directed by Mark Twain from her Ouija board.

Jap Herron was an original novel written in the sense that anyone can tell it was written by an old Mark Twain from past the grave, who wrote it through via the Ouija board. The person who recorded (reliably taking notes down and notes, or maybe more than that depending on your viewpoint) is Emily Grant Hutchings, a lady who had actually compared with Twain 15 years before. In the exchange of letters between them, Twain had offered her a recommendations and, more interestingly she also referred to in one of the letters: "Dolt! Should be protected". According to the comprehensive presentation of Hutchings, "The Coming of Jap Herron", she and a woman called Lola Hays started accepting messages from Twain in 1915, while playing using an Ouija board at a mystical gathering at St. Louis. The practice of tinkering with these unorthodox procedures was not uncommon at the time and appears to have been accepting abstract messages from the past wasn't all that unusual also. The Jap Herron novel came out during a time when the Ouija board exchanges from "Tolerance Worth" by means of St. Louis author Pearl Curran as a co-author with Hutchings (who was present during the initial "interchanges" together with Worth) also was receiving national attention. In reality, as stated in a New York Times article of the time states, Jap Herron was "the third novel of the recent months that has claimed the existence of a dead and created a being who, refusing to give up human activities and has stumbled upon that in the Ouija load up a physical method of expression". It was, however the most well-known creator who was included. The Twain's daughter, Clara Clemens, brought particular issues with the book. She together with the distributers Harper and Brothers, who for many years claimed to own the exclusive rights to the works of Twain filed a lawsuit to stop the distribution.

In the same way, Hutchings and Hays, with the aid of a certain professor Hyslop claimed that Clara's father (after another Ouija board activity) was "in an academic state of suffering due to the difficulty he's facing when trying to get his novel to the market". The case, however did not go to trial since Hutchings ultimately was willing to stop production and destroy any duplicates they found and, in consequence, the remaining copies from the work are astonishingly rare.

Here's the previously reported burning, plainly, New York Times article on the novel in 1917; the year that it was published:

The Ouija board appears to have become an alternative to the typewriter in the creation of fiction. It is the third novel of the last couple of months to claim the authorship of a deceased and gone being that are not ready to abandon human endeavors, seems to locate an Ouija board a viable tool for expression. The last novel is unambiguous in its assertion of its source. The authors responsible for the story, they appear confident that none lesser spirit than the one associated with Mark Twain guided their hands as the story was laid onto the chalkboard. Emily Grant Hutchings and Lola V. Hays are the story's sponsors. Mrs. Hays being the passive receiver whose hands on the pointer were particularly necessary. St. Louis is the location of the incident as well as the site of the literary efforts of the Ouija board, which is the source of"Patience Worth. "Patience Worth" stories. Emily Grant Hutchings, who wrote the introduction to the story, hails located in Hannibal, Mo., the hometown of Mark Twain's youth, and in the story, the spirit of the writer appears to have placed a lot of faith. The long account of how the tale was composed and of the numerous conversations in conversation with Mark Twain through the Ouija board is filled with quotes from his remarks , which sometimes bear a some resemblance to the comedian's signature conversations.

In the course of a night, Patience transformed Pearl Curran from a frightened homemaker afflicted by anxiety-inducing diseases to an active VIP who travelled across the country, exhibiting exhibitions that featured Patience. After a while, Pearl was an attractive, blue-peered woman wearing a trendy gown, would sit in a chair on her Ouija load and her partner, John, recorded Patience's speech in shorthand. People who attended the exhibitions, many of them driving researchers female activists, politicians and writers were able to admit they had witnessed something extraordinary. "Despite all that, I confess to being amused by the experience" Otto Heller, senior member of the Graduate School at Washington University in St. Louis, reviewed several years later.

Through Pearl, Patience asserted to be an unmarried Englishwoman who had moved from Nantucket Island in the late 1600s , only to be killed in the course of an Indian attack. For the last three years, she claimed she would search for an unnatural "crannie" (as as in "skull") in order to assist her in satisfying her burning artistic itch. It was finally discovered in Pearl.

Dorothy Jane Roberts (May 8 1929 - September 5 1984) was an American writer, creator self-declared psychic, self-declared psychic, and soul medium who claimed to channel a vitality-based identity that he referred to as "Seth". The distribution of her Seth writings, referred to in the "Seth Material" established her to be one of the most transcendent people in the field of supernatural phenomena. In the Yale University Library Manuscripts and Archives has a collection of documents titled Jane Roberts Papers (MS 1090) that documents the life and vocation of Jane Roberts, including diaries and correspondence, poetry as well as sound and feature recordings as well as various documents left after her death by Roberts wife and other groups and individuals.

In 1982, writer James Merrill discharged a whole-world epic sonnet that was a total loss of 560-pages. The Changing Light at Sandover The Changing Light at Sandover chronicled 20 years of messages that were managed by the Ouija board in seances led by Merrill and his co-author David Noyes Jackson. Sandover was awarded an award from the National Book Critics Circle Award in 1983, was published in three volumes beginning in 1976. It initially had the ballads for each letter A through Z as well in the book as The Book of Ephraim. It appeared in the collection Divine Comedies, which won the Pulitzer Prize for Poetry in 1977. According to Merrill The spirits contacted him to write and distribute the two parts that followed, Mirabell: Books of Number in 1978 (which received the National Book Award for Poetry) and Scripts for the Pageant in 1980.

Dick Brooks, of the Houdini Museum in Scranton, Pennsylvania, utilizes an Ouija board as an essential component of a paranormal seance-themed presentation.

G. K. Chesterton employed the Ouija board in the course of his teenage period. In 1893, he experienced an eerie feeling of shock and depression, and throughout the time Chesterton looked into various avenues for the Ouija board, and was enthralled by the mystery of.

Early squeeze releases stated the idea that Vincent Furnier's stage as well as the band's title "Alice Cooper" was decided upon following an evening with an Ouija Board, during which it was discovered it was believed that Furnier was the reincarnation of a witch from the 17th century with this name. Alice Cooper later uncovered that was just thinking about the first name that came to his head as he was examining the name of another band in his band.

On the 25th of July 2007 airing broadcast of the radio paranormal program Coast to Coast AM, host George Noory endeavored to complete live Ouija board investigation of on national radio, despite the objections of one his guests. Following the retelling of an incident that ended in 2000 and observing of unusual events that occurred, Noory scratched off the trial.

Previous Italian Premier Romano Prodi asserted under pledge that in a séance which was held in 1978 along with various teachers in Bologna's University of Bologna, the "apparition" of Giorgio La Pira utilized a Ouija to spell out the name of the street where Aldo Moro was imprisoned to be held by Red Brigades. According to Peter Popham of The Independent: "Everyone here has since some time ago recognized that Prodi's Ouija story was in fact an untrue and bizarre attempt to conceal the identity of his source, which is most likely an Italian from Bologna's infamous extreme left underground, which he swearing to protect."

The Mars Volta composed their collection Bedlam in Goliath (2008) due to their tense experience to the Ouija board. According to their tale (composed for by a writer, Jeremy Robert Johnson), Omar

Rodriguez Lopez acquired one during his trip to Jerusalem. The board initially told the story, which later became the subject of the collection. Some interesting incidents that were supposedly connected to this movement took place during when the collections were being recorded. The studio was overflowing, one the principal architects of the collection suffered an emotional breakdown, the hardware began to malfunction and Cedric Bixler-Zavala's leg was injured. In response to these terrible events, the group wrapped their Ouija board.

In the case of homicide that was the case of Joshua Tucker, his mom wanted to know if he'd completed the murders under the control of the Devil and was discovered using an Ouija board.

The case was brought to London during 1994 the sentenced murderer Stephen Young was allowed a hearing after it was found out that four attendees had led an Ouija seance to load up and "reached" the man who was killed who identified Young as the murderer. Young was accused for a moment of during his trial and sentenced to life imprisonment.

Aleister Crowley displayed a remarkable respect for the The Ouija board and believed it played an insignificant part in his supernatural activities. Jane Wolfe, who lived alongside Crowley within his amusing Abbey of Thelema also made use of this Ouija board. She attributes some of her most intense interactions to this method. Crowley also discussed her experience with the Ouija board with one of his students, and one of the most energetic of them was Frater Achad (Charles Stansfeld Jones) It is often mentioned in their letters, which are never published. In 1917, Achad attempted a variety of things using the board, including method of summoning Angels in lieu of Elementals. In a letter, Crowley stated to Jones: "Your Ouija board analysis can be enjoyable. You realize how wonderful it is, but I believe that things improve tremendously through experience. I believe you should remain with one divine participant, and let the supernatural arrangements expand." Through the years the two turned out to be so enthralled by the Ouija Board that they began to think about ways to advertise their own designs. Their conversation culminated in a letter dated 21 February 1919 in which Crowley writes to Jones, "Re: Ouija Board. I'm willing to grant you the benefit of 10 percent of my net gain. You are, if you agree or not, the owner of the legal protection of the ideas, and the display of the copyright outline. I presume that this will be a good idea for you. I'd like to offer you the opportunity to read the information over the course of one week." On March 1, Crowley made a song to Achad to make him more clear, "I'll brainstorm another name for Ouija.

"There is however an effective way to use this instrument to obtain what you desire which is to carry out the entire procedure in a sacred circle, which means that unwelcome foreigners cannot interfere. Then, you can use the correct magickal invocation to attract within your circle only the spirit you're looking for. It's fairly simple to achieve this. A few easy steps are all you require and I'll be delighted to offer the same, for free to anyone who wants to use. "

Chapter 15: What To Do With An Ouija Board

Once you've bought or made the Ouija board, it's time to get it in use.

1. First of all, you must have at minimum 3 or four individuals.

* Each participant will be assigned distinct roles to fulfill in the event.

* Documenters are people in your group that is not part of the actual conversation in the spirit, and won't be touching the coin , glass. Planchette.

It is expected to record everything that is spoken by group members or the spirit in the course of the session.

"The documenter" the person who should keep an encyclopedia of the Holy Bible handy. The Documenter should have a strong belief in God and should be firmly spiritual.

* When I was a teenager typically, I would turn into a recorder. It's probably the most important position in the team.

* A medium is a person who may be asked questions in the presence of the Spirit.

* The Medium must be someone who is serious and knows the right is appropriate to inquire about and which to not ask since certain questions could anger the spirit or leave it confused.

* The Participants are others who touch the glass, the coin and the Planchette.

* Participants are required to remain for a long time.

2. It is important to ensure that everyone is close to that Ouija board. The Documenter could be a bit away as her/his job is to record.

3. Lighting a candle is a good idea and place it next to the Planchette to ensure that everyone can read the words that are written on it. The room must be dark, and no doors or windows should be open. This is done in order to make sure that you

aren't only a breeze entering through an unclosed window.

4. Pray this prayer:

As a sign Christ Jesus Christ, we ask to be protected from evil. Nothing other than light, goodness and love surround us on this day. Only the divine energies and spirits of heaven and light come into this world. We pray to the Holy Spirit that we beg to protect us by the bright glow of your loving embrace, shielding us from deceit and malice. By the grace Jesus Christ, in the name of Jesus Christ we banish all negative energies, evil spirits and evil spirits from the area.

Because God does not have a mind that is fearful, but love and power. We also have an enlightened mind. Amen.

5. Then, all participants and the Moderator should place their fingers on the coin or grip the Planchette.

6. The next suggestion in many websites is to remain quiet and wait for something to happen to you. This is not the case!

Because you don't know what could happen.

7. Instead, speak the following lines as groups.

Any HOLY Spirit that is passing by near Us, Please come to us.

8. Repeat those exact words for the next couple of minutes. This is an extremely fast way to accomplish things.

9. After a few minutes, if you feel a breeze blowing on you or the candle's flame begins acting strangely, changing hues or changing in size. Also, if you hear an ominous sound that is heard by all or if you have similar experience, the Medium needs to inquire.

Are you there, Holy Spirit?

10. A response will follow. If not, go back to the steps 6-8.

Then, you can request the spirit to affirm its existence by shifting it's candle's light in a particular manner.

That's the end of it. The spirit is now arrived, you can ask questions using the medium. It is important to prepare. Even though other people may also ask questions, it is always preferred.

After you are done with your queries Here's how to return the item to the place it came from:

1. When you're done with the session, say

Holy Spirit, please leave US now

2. If the spirit is saying yes or you are feeling it, you are in a room, leave, set the Planchette down , or remove the coin from the board. Ouija board.

3. After that, you can conclude with this prayer

As a sign Christ's name Jesus Christ we command all spirits, energies and entities within this area to return from the place from which they came. We pray for the Holy Spirit be with this area and the inhabitants living there, sanitizing this house with the holy light and keeping evil out of the house. In Jesus's name, we pray. Amen.

4. If the spirit doesn't want to leave, do not be afraid, just pick up the coin and place it away. If you're using a Planchette then smash it onto the board's surface and place it in a safe place, and then pray the previously stated prayer.

Always keep your eyes closed and OPEN With a prayer!

5. Turn on the lights and spend the remainder of the evening sharing your memories.

Tips to Make Sure That Things Don't Go awry

1. Always pray prior to and following the session.

2. Always have holy water along with a cross and Bible near you in case of emergency.

3. Be sure that members of your group are not disrespectful of the spirit. A good spirit

may get annoyed by idiots and should someone upset an individual spirit everything that happens is entirely the fault of the person. Avoid inviting people who are irritable.

4. Do not utilize your Ouija board in a location that is known for its violent manifestations or in areas where there has been a tragic incident.

5. Do not play on playing with the Ouija Board alone. This increases your chance of being attracted to.

6. Always dispose of the Ouija board following the ritual. Then tear it apart and sprinkle holy water on it. You can either bury it or put it in a holy spot (if it is possible).

7. Don't put the Planchette on the board when you're not working with it.

8. Don't ask spirits why it passed away.

9. Faith in God and the All-powerful.

10. Don't try to make someone other than yourself believe in this belief. Sure , it's an

enjoyable experience that makes believers out of people , but it could also go horribly wrong.

We'll be discussing it on the next episode.

What do you do when things go wrong?

Sometimes things can happen to go wrong. Check this link:

This isn't the only spot where you can run into terrifying stories.

Here are some ideas to repair things in the event that they go wrong:

1. Make a call to a priest and get the area cleaned.

2. Take apart and tear up the Ouija board and cut off the pieces. Sprinkle holy water over it, and then put it in a grave in a place far from the glare of civilization. OR

3. It is recommended to burn your Ouija board, along with the herbs like sage. This will transform your board to ashes, and allow you to live your life in peace

4. When you, or someone around you in your family is experiencing an unusual or strange experience Get help immediately from the priest of your church.

5. If you find yourself in a situation where things are not going as planned and one does end up being trapped, leave it to the professionals (priests) manage the situation.

6. Do not talk to anything that is manifesting itself. That is how they are able to become attracted to you.

7. Don't be afraid. That is why it is important to keep the Bible with you whenever things turn sour on your Ouija board.

8. Be mindful of God and trust in his power. He is stronger than any other thing in the world. Be aware of that and be loyal.

9. When the experience isn't working Do not try a second session in the same spot or with the person who was affected. This can result in more issues.

Last but not least, keep in mind that the spirits who communicate via these mediums may not be as powerful as they say.

They can influence your mind, however the very first step they take is to study your thoughts, and in turn create situations to make you feel scared. They may occasionally make use of names for more powerful negative forces to scare you, however they're really just a bunch of tricker souls.

If something really sinister comes through, you'll be able to recognize that it is:

Spirits that are evil emit extremely unpleasant smells and are extremely hazardous. If you are using the same board , which has caused trouble previously, you'll expose yourself to even more dangerous creatures. This guide isn't enough to warn you about the horrors that are likely to follow.

Conclusion

It is a fact that the Ouija board is definitely not a subject to debate or being associated with dark. This book has hopefully given you enough information to assist you in making smart choices regarding the Ouija board is concerned.

Thank you for buying this book!

I hope that this book has been useful in helping you discover the darker aspect that lies behind the Ouija board through the disturbing stories you've learned within the pages.

www.ingramcontent.com/pod-product-compliance
Lightning Source LLC
Chambersburg PA
CBHW050407120526
44590CB00015B/1868